Sourdough Sweet Recipes Book

60 Delectable Dessert Recipes and Tips for Cakes, Pancakes, Donuts, Croissants, and More

Leah Guda

This book belongs to

THE LIBRARY OF:

- -

Thanks ever so much to each of my cherished readers for investing the time to read this book!

I know you could have picked from many other books, but you chose this one. So, a big thanks for reading all the way to the end. If you enjoyed this book or received value from it, I'd like to ask you for a favor. Please take a few minutes to *post an honest and heartfelt review on Amazon.com.* Your support does make a difference and helps to benefit other people.

Thanks!

Table of Contents

Summary

"The Unique Charm of Sourdough Desserts: Sourdough desserts have a unique charm that sets them apart from other types of desserts. The use of sourdough starter in these desserts adds a tangy and complex flavor profile that is both intriguing and delicious. This distinct flavor is a result of the fermentation process that the sourdough starter undergoes, which creates a natural acidity that enhances the taste of the dessert.

One of the key benefits of using sourdough in desserts is its ability to create a light and airy texture. The natural yeast in the sourdough starter helps to leaven the dessert, resulting in a soft and fluffy consistency. This is particularly evident in sourdough cakes and pastries, where the sourdough starter acts as a natural leavening agent, replacing the need for commercial yeast or baking powder.

In addition to its unique flavor and texture, sourdough desserts also offer a range of health benefits. The fermentation process that the sourdough starter undergoes helps to break down the gluten in the flour, making it easier to digest for those with gluten sensitivities. This makes sourdough desserts a great option for individuals who are looking for gluten-free or low-gluten alternatives.

Furthermore, sourdough desserts are often made with natural and wholesome ingredients. The use of sourdough starter, which is essentially a mixture of flour and water that has been fermented, means that these desserts are free from artificial additives and preservatives. This makes them a healthier choice compared to commercially produced desserts that are often loaded with sugar and artificial ingredients.

Sourdough desserts also offer a wide variety of options for experimentation and creativity. From sourdough bread pudding to sourdough cinnamon rolls, there are endless possibilities when it comes to incorporating sourdough into desserts. The tangy flavor of the sourdough starter pairs well with a range of ingredients, such as fruits, nuts, and spices, allowing for endless flavor combinations.

Overall, the unique charm of sourdough desserts lies in their distinct flavor, light and airy texture, health benefits, and versatility. Whether you are a fan of tangy flavors or simply looking for a healthier alternative to traditional desserts, sourdough desserts are sure to satisfy your cravings and leave you wanting more. So why not give them a try and experience the delightful charm of sourdough desserts for yourself?"

"Overview of Long-Leavening Baking of Sourdough Desserts: Long-leavening baking of sourdough desserts is a unique and traditional method of baking that involves using a sourdough starter as the leavening agent instead of commercial yeast. This process requires a longer fermentation time, typically ranging from 12 to 24 hours, allowing the natural yeasts and bacteria present in the sourdough starter to slowly ferment the dough and develop complex flavors.

The use of sourdough in baking has been practiced for centuries, with its origins dating back to ancient Egypt. It was a common method of leavening bread before the commercialization of yeast. However, in recent years, sourdough has gained popularity not only in bread baking but also in the creation of delicious and unique sourdough desserts.

The long-leavening process of sourdough desserts begins with the preparation of a sourdough starter, which is a mixture of flour and water that is left to ferment for several days. During this fermentation period, wild yeasts and lactobacilli bacteria naturally present in the environment and on the flour begin to colonize the mixture, creating a living culture that will be used to leaven the dough.

Once the sourdough starter is ready, it is incorporated into the dessert dough, along with other ingredients such as flour, sugar, eggs, and butter. The dough is then left to ferment for an extended period, allowing the sourdough starter to work its magic. This slow fermentation process not only leavens the dough but also imparts a distinct tangy flavor and a light, airy texture to the final dessert.

One of the key benefits of long-leavening baking of sourdough desserts is the enhanced flavor profile it brings to the table. The natural fermentation process of the sourdough starter creates a depth of flavor that cannot be replicated with commercial yeast. The tanginess of the sourdough adds a pleasant and unique taste to the desserts, making them stand out from their commercially leavened counterparts.

Furthermore, the long fermentation time also contributes to the development of a more digestible and nutritious dessert. The fermentation process breaks down complex carbohydrates and proteins, making them easier to digest. It also increases the bioavailability of certain nutrients, making them more accessible to our bodies.

In addition to the flavor and nutritional benefits, long-leavening baking of sourdough desserts also offers a more sustainable and environmentally friendly approach to baking. By relying on natural fermentation instead of commercial yeast, it reduces the need for energy"

"Purpose and Scope of Sourdough Desserts: The purpose and scope of sourdough desserts encompass a wide range of objectives and possibilities. Sourdough, a fermented dough made from a combination of flour and water, has been traditionally associated with bread-making. However, in recent years, its application in the realm of desserts has gained significant attention and popularity.

One of the primary purposes of sourdough desserts is to explore and showcase the unique flavors and textures that can be achieved through the fermentation process. The natural yeasts and bacteria present in sourdough starter contribute to the development of complex flavors, tanginess, and a subtle hint of acidity. These characteristics can add depth and sophistication to desserts, elevating them beyond the ordinary.

Furthermore, sourdough desserts offer an alternative for individuals with gluten sensitivities or intolerances. The fermentation process breaks down gluten proteins, making them more digestible for those who may otherwise struggle with gluten-containing desserts. This opens up a whole new world of possibilities for individuals who have been limited in their dessert choices due to dietary restrictions.

The scope of sourdough desserts is vast and diverse. From classic favorites like sourdough chocolate cake and sourdough cinnamon rolls to more innovative creations like sourdough ice cream and sourdough donuts, there is no shortage of options to explore. Sourdough can be incorporated into various dessert components, such as cakes, cookies, pastries, and even custards, allowing for endless experimentation and creativity.

Moreover, sourdough desserts provide an opportunity to reduce food waste. Sourdough starter requires regular feeding and maintenance, resulting in excess discard that would otherwise go to waste. By incorporating this discard into desserts, bakers can minimize their environmental impact and contribute to a more sustainable food system.

In addition to the culinary aspects, sourdough desserts also offer a unique cultural and historical significance. Sourdough has been a staple in many cultures for centuries, and incorporating it into desserts allows for a connection to traditional baking practices and heritage. It provides an opportunity to celebrate and preserve culinary traditions while also embracing innovation and modernity.

In conclusion, the purpose and scope of sourdough desserts extend far beyond simply satisfying a sweet tooth. They offer a platform for exploring unique flavors, catering to dietary restrictions, reducing food waste, and connecting to cultural and historical roots. With its versatility and potential for creativity, sourdough desserts have become a fascinating and exciting realm within the world of baking and pastry."

"Navigating through Sourdough Desserts Book: Navigating through the Sourdough Desserts Book is an exciting and delicious journey into the world of baking with sourdough. This book is a comprehensive guide that provides detailed instructions and recipes for creating a wide variety of mouthwatering desserts using sourdough as a key ingredient.

The book begins with an introduction to sourdough and its unique characteristics that make it a fantastic addition to desserts. It explains how sourdough adds depth of flavor, enhances texture, and improves the overall quality of baked goods. The authors also provide tips on how to maintain and care for a sourdough starter, ensuring that readers have a reliable and active sourdough culture to work with.

As you delve deeper into the book, you will find a diverse range of dessert recipes that showcase the versatility of sourdough. From classic favorites like sourdough chocolate cake and sourdough cinnamon rolls to more innovative creations like sourdough lemon bars and sourdough blueberry muffins, there is something to satisfy every sweet tooth.

Each recipe is accompanied by clear and concise instructions, making it easy for both novice and experienced bakers to follow along. The authors also provide helpful tips and tricks throughout the book, sharing their expertise and insights to ensure success in the kitchen. Whether it's advice on how to achieve the perfect rise or suggestions for creative flavor combinations, these additional tidbits of information add value to the overall baking experience.

One of the standout features of this book is the inclusion of stunning photographs that accompany each recipe. These visuals not only showcase the finished desserts in all their glory but also provide inspiration and motivation for readers to try their hand at recreating these delectable treats. The photographs capture the textures, colors, and presentation of the desserts, making it impossible to resist the urge to grab a mixing bowl and get baking.

In addition to the recipes, the book also includes a section on troubleshooting common issues that may arise when working with sourdough. This troubleshooting guide is a valuable resource for bakers, as it offers solutions to problems such as a sluggish starter or a dense cake. By addressing these challenges head-on, the authors empower readers to overcome any obstacles and achieve bakery-worthy results.

Overall, navigating through the Sourdough Desserts Book is a delightful and informative experience. It not only provides a wealth of delicious recipes but also equips readers with the knowledge and skills to confidently incorporate sourdough into their baking repertoire. Whether you're a seasoned baker looking to expand your"

"Understanding Sourdough Fermentation of Sourdough Desserts: Understanding the process of sourdough fermentation in the context of sourdough desserts involves delving into the intricate world of microbiology and the art of baking. Sourdough fermentation is a natural process that occurs when a mixture of flour and water is left to ferment, allowing wild yeast and bacteria to colonize and thrive. This fermentation process not only imparts a unique tangy flavor to the dough but also enhances its texture and nutritional value.

The key players in sourdough fermentation are the wild yeast and lactic acid bacteria. These microorganisms are naturally present in the environment, particularly in the air and on the surface of grains. When flour and water are combined, these microorganisms begin to feed on the carbohydrates present in the flour, breaking them down into simpler sugars. The wild yeast then consumes these sugars and produces carbon dioxide gas as a byproduct, causing the dough to rise. Simultaneously, the lactic acid bacteria convert the sugars into lactic acid, which contributes to the characteristic sour taste of sourdough.

The fermentation process of sourdough desserts differs slightly from that of traditional sourdough bread. While bread dough typically undergoes a long fermentation period, sourdough desserts often require a shorter fermentation time to achieve the desired flavor and texture. This is because the acidity produced during fermentation can affect the structure and taste of the final product. Therefore, bakers must carefully monitor the fermentation process to strike the right balance between flavor development and maintaining the desired texture.

In addition to flavor and texture, sourdough fermentation also has a significant impact on the nutritional profile of sourdough desserts. The fermentation process breaks down complex carbohydrates, making them more easily digestible. It also increases the bioavailability of certain nutrients, such as iron, zinc, and magnesium, making them more accessible to the body. This makes sourdough desserts a healthier alternative to their non-fermented counterparts.

To successfully incorporate sourdough fermentation into desserts, bakers must understand the factors that influence the fermentation process. Temperature, hydration level, and the type of flour used all play crucial roles in determining the speed and outcome of fermentation. Bakers must also consider the specific requirements of the dessert they are making, as different recipes may call for different fermentation techniques and durations.

In conclusion, understanding the sourdough fermentation process in the context of sourdough desserts requires a deep appreciation for the science and art of baking. The interplay between wild yeast, lactic acid bacteria, and"

"The Role of Wild Yeast and Lactic Acid Bacteria of Sourdough Desserts: The Role of Wild Yeast and Lactic Acid Bacteria in the Fermentation Process of Sourdough Desserts

Sourdough desserts have gained popularity in recent years due to their unique flavor profile and health benefits. Unlike traditional desserts that rely on commercial yeast for leavening, sourdough desserts utilize a combination of wild yeast and lactic acid bacteria to undergo fermentation. This fermentation process not only imparts a distinct tangy flavor to the desserts but also enhances their nutritional value.

Wild yeast, also known as Saccharomyces cerevisiae, is naturally present in the environment, particularly on the surface of grains and fruits. When incorporated into sourdough desserts, wild yeast feeds on the carbohydrates present in the dough, converting them into carbon dioxide and alcohol through the process of alcoholic fermentation. The carbon dioxide produced by wild yeast creates air pockets within the dough, resulting in a light and airy texture in the final product. Additionally, the alcohol produced during fermentation evaporates during baking, leaving behind the unique flavor notes associated with sourdough desserts.

Lactic acid bacteria, on the other hand, play a crucial role in the souring of the dough. These bacteria, including species such as Lactobacillus sanfranciscensis and Lactobacillus brevis, produce lactic acid as a byproduct of their metabolism. The lactic acid lowers the pH of the dough, creating an acidic environment that inhibits the growth of harmful bacteria and molds. This natural preservation effect not only extends the shelf life of sourdough desserts but also contributes to their characteristic tangy taste.

In addition to their leavening and souring abilities, wild yeast and lactic acid bacteria also enhance the nutritional value of sourdough desserts. The fermentation process breaks down complex carbohydrates into simpler forms, making them more easily digestible. This increases the bioavailability of nutrients, such as vitamins and minerals, present in the dough. Furthermore, the presence of lactic acid bacteria in sourdough desserts promotes the growth of beneficial gut bacteria, which can improve digestion and overall gut health.

It is important to note that the composition and activity of wild yeast and lactic acid bacteria can vary depending on factors such as the geographical location, type of flour used, and fermentation conditions. Therefore, bakers often cultivate and maintain their own sourdough starters, which are mixtures of flour and water that capture and promote the growth of specific strains of wild yeast and lactic acid bacteria."

"Benefits of Long-Leavening Process of Sourdough Desserts: The long-leavening process of sourdough desserts offers numerous benefits that contribute to their unique taste, texture, and overall quality. This traditional method involves allowing the dough to ferment for an extended period, typically overnight or even up to several days, before baking. While this process requires patience and planning, the end result is well worth the wait.

One of the primary advantages of the long-leavening process is the development of complex flavors. As the dough ferments, the natural yeasts and bacteria present in the sourdough starter break down the carbohydrates and proteins, releasing a range of aromatic compounds. These compounds contribute to the distinct tangy and slightly sour taste that is characteristic of sourdough desserts. The longer fermentation time allows for a more pronounced flavor profile, resulting in a more satisfying and enjoyable eating experience.

In addition to enhancing the flavor, the long-leavening process also improves the texture of sourdough desserts. The fermentation process breaks down the gluten in the dough, making it easier to digest and resulting in a lighter and more tender crumb. This is particularly beneficial for individuals with gluten sensitivities or intolerances, as the longer fermentation time reduces the gluten content in the final product. Furthermore, the production of lactic acid during fermentation helps to soften the dough, resulting in a moist and chewy texture that is highly desirable in desserts such as breads, cakes, and pastries.

Another advantage of the long-leavening process is its impact on the nutritional profile of sourdough desserts. The fermentation process increases the bioavailability of certain nutrients, making them easier for the body to absorb. For example, the phytic acid present in grains is broken down during fermentation, releasing minerals such as iron, zinc, and magnesium. This not only enhances the nutritional value of the desserts but also improves their digestibility.

Furthermore, the long-leavening process of sourdough desserts has been found to have potential health benefits. The lactic acid bacteria produced during fermentation have probiotic properties, which can promote a healthy gut microbiome and improve digestion. Additionally, the slower fermentation process allows for better control of blood sugar levels, making sourdough desserts a suitable option for individuals with diabetes or those looking to manage their blood sugar levels.

In conclusion, the long-leavening process of sourdough desserts offers a multitude of benefits. From the development of complex flavors to the improvement of texture and nutritional value, this traditional method elevates the overall quality of the final"

"Characteristics of Sourdough Baked Goods: Sourdough baked goods are a unique and flavorful type of bread and pastry that are made using a natural fermentation process. This process involves the use of a sourdough starter, which is a mixture of flour and water that has been left to ferment and develop a complex network of wild yeast and bacteria. These microorganisms are what give sourdough its distinct tangy flavor and chewy texture.

One of the key characteristics of sourdough baked goods is their rich and complex flavor profile. The fermentation process allows the wild yeast and bacteria to break down the carbohydrates in the flour, resulting in the production of lactic acid and acetic acid. These acids contribute to the sour taste of the bread and give it a depth of flavor that is often lacking in commercially produced breads.

Another characteristic of sourdough baked goods is their unique texture. The wild yeast and bacteria in the sourdough starter produce carbon dioxide gas as they feed on the carbohydrates in the flour. This gas gets trapped in the dough, causing it to rise and develop a light and airy crumb. Additionally, the acids produced during fermentation help to break down the proteins in the flour, resulting in a more elastic and chewy texture.

Sourdough baked goods also have a longer shelf life compared to other types of bread. The lactic acid produced during fermentation acts as a natural preservative, inhibiting the growth of mold and extending the freshness of the bread. This means that sourdough bread can stay fresh for several days without the need for added preservatives.

Furthermore, sourdough baked goods are often considered to be more nutritious than other types of bread. The fermentation process helps to break down the phytic acid found in the bran of the flour, making the nutrients more bioavailable and easier to digest. Additionally, the longer fermentation time allows for the development of beneficial bacteria, which can aid in digestion and promote a healthy gut microbiome.

In conclusion, sourdough baked goods are characterized by their rich and complex flavor, unique texture, extended shelf life, and nutritional benefits. The natural fermentation process used to make sourdough bread and pastries results in a product that is not only delicious but also healthier and more easily digestible. Whether it's a crusty loaf of sourdough bread or a flaky sourdough croissant, these baked goods are sure to satisfy both the taste buds and the stomach."

"Crafting Your Own Sourdough Starter of Sourdough Desserts: Crafting your own sourdough starter is a rewarding and fulfilling process that allows you to create a wide variety of delicious sourdough desserts. Sourdough desserts have gained popularity in recent years due to their unique tangy flavor and the health benefits associated with sourdough fermentation.

To begin crafting your own sourdough starter, you will need just a few simple ingredients: flour, water, and time. The process starts by combining equal parts flour and water in a clean container. It is important to use unbleached flour, as bleached flour may contain chemicals that can inhibit the growth of the natural yeast present in the flour. Once the flour and water are mixed together, cover the container with a clean cloth or plastic wrap and let it sit at room temperature for 24 hours.

After 24 hours, you will begin to see some activity in your sourdough starter. Bubbles will start to form on the surface, indicating that the natural yeast in the flour is becoming active and fermenting the mixture. At this point, you will need to discard half of the starter and feed it with fresh flour and water. This process, known as ""feeding,"" helps to maintain a healthy balance of yeast and bacteria in the starter.

Feeding your sourdough starter is a crucial step in the process, as it provides the yeast with the nutrients it needs to thrive. To feed your starter, simply discard half of the mixture and add equal parts flour and water. Stir the mixture well to incorporate the new ingredients and cover it again. Repeat this process every 24 hours for the next few days, discarding half of the starter and feeding it with fresh flour and water.

As your sourdough starter continues to ferment, it will develop a distinct sour smell and tangy flavor. This is a sign that the natural yeast and bacteria in the starter are working together to create a complex and flavorful mixture. Once your starter is fully matured, usually after about a week of daily feedings, it is ready to be used in sourdough dessert recipes.

Sourdough desserts offer a unique twist on traditional baked goods. The tangy flavor of the sourdough adds depth and complexity to desserts like bread pudding, pancakes, and even chocolate cake. The natural fermentation process also helps to break down gluten in the flour, making sourdough desserts easier to digest for those with gluten sensitivities.

When using your sourdough starter in dessert recipes, it is important to remember"

"Feeding and Maintaining a Healthy Starter of Sourdough Desserts: Feeding and maintaining a healthy starter for sourdough desserts is a crucial step in ensuring the success and quality of your baked goods. A sourdough starter is a mixture of flour and water that contains wild yeast and bacteria. These microorganisms are responsible for the fermentation process that gives sourdough its distinct flavor and texture.

To begin, you will need to create your sourdough starter. This can be done by combining equal parts of flour and water in a clean container. It is important to use unbleached flour, as bleached flour may contain chemicals that can inhibit the growth of the wild yeast and bacteria.

Once combined, cover the container loosely with a clean cloth or plastic wrap and let it sit at room temperature for 24 hours.

After 24 hours, you will notice some activity in your starter. Bubbles may have formed on the surface, indicating that fermentation has begun. At this point, you will need to discard half of the starter and feed it with fresh flour and water. Discarding half of the starter helps to maintain a manageable size and ensures that the yeast and bacteria have enough food to thrive.

To feed your starter, remove half of the existing starter from the container and discard it. Then, add equal parts of flour and water to the remaining starter. For example, if you have 100 grams of starter, discard 50 grams and add 50 grams each of flour and water. Mix well to incorporate the flour and water into the starter, making sure there are no dry pockets.

Once the starter is fed, cover it again and let it sit at room temperature for another 24 hours. During this time, the yeast and bacteria will continue to ferment and multiply, creating a stronger and more active starter. You may notice that the starter becomes more bubbly and fragrant as it matures.

Feeding your starter should be done regularly to keep it healthy and active. Depending on the temperature and activity level of your starter, you may need to feed it every 12 to 24 hours. It is important to observe your starter and adjust the feeding schedule accordingly. If your starter is very active and bubbly, it may need to be fed more frequently. On the other hand, if your starter is sluggish and not showing much activity, it may need less frequent feedings.

In addition to regular feedings, it is important to maintain the hydration level of your starter. The hydration level refers to the ratio of flour to water in the starter."

"Troubleshooting Common Starter Issues of Sourdough Desserts:

Sourdough desserts have gained popularity in recent years due to their unique flavor and texture. However, working with a sourdough starter can sometimes be challenging, especially when it comes to baking desserts. If you're experiencing issues with your sourdough starter when making desserts, here are some common problems and troubleshooting tips to help you achieve the perfect results.

1. Lack of Rise: One of the most common issues when using a sourdough starter in desserts is a lack of rise. This can result in dense and heavy desserts that don't have the desired light and fluffy texture. There are a few reasons why this may happen. Firstly, your starter may not be active enough. To fix this, try feeding your starter more frequently and at regular intervals. This will ensure that the yeast in your starter is active and ready to leaven your desserts. Additionally, make sure you're using the right amount of starter in your recipe. Too little starter can result in a lack of rise, so be sure to follow the recipe instructions carefully.

2. Overly Sour Flavor: Sourdough desserts are known for their tangy flavor, but sometimes the sourness can be overpowering. If your desserts are turning out too sour, there are a few things you can do to balance the flavor. Firstly, consider reducing the amount of sourdough starter in your recipe. Using less starter will result in a milder flavor. Additionally, you can try adding a small amount of sugar or honey to your recipe to counteract the sourness. Finally, make sure you're giving

your starter enough time to ferment before using it in your desserts. A longer fermentation period can help develop a more balanced flavor.

3. Dense and Gummy Texture: Another common issue when using a sourdough starter in desserts is a dense and gummy texture. This can be frustrating, especially when you're expecting a light and airy dessert. One possible cause of this problem is overmixing the batter. When working with sourdough, it's important to mix the ingredients just until they're combined. Overmixing can develop the gluten in the flour, resulting in a dense and gummy texture. Another possible cause is using a low-protein flour. Sourdough desserts require a flour with a higher protein content to help create structure and a lighter texture. Make sure you're using the right type of flour for your recipes.

4. Slow Fer"

"Storing and Reviving Sourdough Starter of Sourdough Desserts: Storing and reviving a sourdough starter is an essential step in maintaining a healthy and active culture that can be used to make a variety of delicious sourdough desserts. Sourdough starters are living organisms that consist of wild yeast and lactobacilli bacteria, which work together to ferment the dough and give it its distinct tangy flavor.

To store a sourdough starter, it is important to first feed it with equal parts flour and water to ensure that it has enough nutrients to stay alive. This feeding process should be done regularly, ideally every 12 hours, to keep the starter active and prevent it from becoming too acidic or developing off-flavors. Once the starter has been fed, it can be transferred to a clean and airtight container, such as a glass jar or a plastic container with a tight-fitting lid.

When storing a sourdough starter, it is crucial to keep it in a cool and stable environment, preferably between 40-50°F (4-10°C). This temperature range helps to slow down the fermentation process and allows the starter to maintain its vitality for a longer period of time. It is also important to avoid exposing the starter to extreme temperatures, as this can kill the yeast and bacteria.

Reviving a sourdough starter is a simple process that involves feeding the dormant culture to reactivate its fermentation activity. To do this, take a small amount of the stored starter and discard the rest. Then, feed the remaining starter with equal parts flour and water, just as you would when storing it. Allow the revived starter to sit at room temperature for a few hours, or until it becomes bubbly and active again. This process may take anywhere from a few hours to a couple of days, depending on the condition of the starter.

Once the sourdough starter has been revived, it can be used to make a wide range of sourdough desserts. From classic sourdough bread to pancakes, waffles, muffins, and even cakes, the possibilities are endless. The sourdough starter adds a unique flavor and texture to these desserts, making them more complex and flavorful than their traditional counterparts.

In conclusion, storing and reviving a sourdough starter is a crucial step in maintaining a healthy and active culture that can be used to create a variety of delicious sourdough desserts. By following the proper feeding and storage techniques, as well as reviving the starter when necessary, you can ensure that your sourd"

"Overview of Sourdough Donuts and Rolls: Sourdough donuts and rolls are a delicious and unique twist on traditional baked goods. Made with a sourdough starter, these treats have a distinct tangy flavor and a soft, fluffy texture that sets them apart from regular donuts and rolls.

The process of making sourdough donuts and rolls starts with creating a sourdough starter. This is a mixture of flour and water that is left to ferment for several days, allowing wild yeast and bacteria to develop. The fermentation process gives the dough its characteristic tangy flavor and helps to create a light and airy texture.

Once the sourdough starter is ready, it is combined with additional flour, sugar, eggs, and butter to create a dough. This dough is then kneaded and left to rise for several hours, allowing the yeast to work its magic and create air pockets in the dough. The longer the dough is allowed to rise, the more flavorful and tender the final product will be.

After the dough has risen, it is shaped into donuts or rolls and fried or baked until golden brown. The frying method creates a crispy exterior while the baking method results in a slightly softer texture. Both methods yield delicious results, so it ultimately comes down to personal preference.

Sourdough donuts can be enjoyed plain, dusted with powdered sugar, or glazed with a sweet icing. They can also be filled with various fillings such as jam, custard, or Nutella, adding an extra layer of flavor and indulgence. Sourdough rolls, on the other hand, are perfect for sandwiches or as a side to soups and stews. Their tangy flavor adds a unique twist to any meal.

One of the great things about sourdough donuts and rolls is their versatility. They can be made with different types of flour, such as whole wheat or rye, to add depth of flavor and nutritional value. They can also be flavored with various spices, extracts, or zests to create different taste profiles. The possibilities are endless when it comes to experimenting with sourdough donuts and rolls.

In addition to their delicious taste, sourdough donuts and rolls also offer some health benefits. The fermentation process involved in making sourdough helps to break down gluten, making it easier to digest for those with gluten sensitivities. The natural yeast and bacteria in sourdough also contribute to a healthier gut microbiome, promoting better digestion and overall gut health.

Overall, sourdough donuts"

Chapter 1

Introduction

Welcome to this recipe book entirely dedicated to preparing desserts with the use of our dearest friend - and why not, ally - in the kitchen, the mother yeast!

As you well know, sourdough is often linked to the preparation of bread and sometimes pizza. But why is its use so strict?

Obviously, bread is one of the oldest types of food, as is mother yeast.

There is information on sourdough bread before the first century. In Italy, bread was prepared by housewives, thanks to the use of mother yeast. This yeast was created from the maceration of fresh fruit and was a source of housewives' pride; They took great care of it: from the yeast quality derive primary characteristics, as well as the shelf life of the bread itself, which ranged from 7 to 9 days minimum! It was essential to ensure the livelihood of farmers and shepherds in the weeks they spent away from home, working in the fields on the hills or in the pastures.

And here is how this tradition and this pride have come down to the present day.

If you are reading this book there are two options: either you are a mother yeast fan, and you are keeping at least 30/40 g of it in the fridge, or you are curious and want to immerse yourself in this new world!

I have good news for both cases: if you are a sourdough fan and you already know how it works, you absolutely have to read the gourmet pizzas recipes I included in the book entitled "Authentic Italian Pizza: the cookbook". You'll find 45 dough recipes for all tastes, as well as endless possibilities for gourmet toppings, plus one associated with each dough!

On the other hand, if you are curious and can't wait to start venturing in this way, I recommend that you first start studying the ingredients and the important factors of leavening, such as temperature and hydration. In fact, in the book "Authentic Italian Pizza" I dealt with all the elements that make up creating an exquisite homemade pizza, starting from the choice of ingredients, the secrets for correct leavening, passing through the topping and cooking of the pizza, both in the baking tin and classic round pizza.

Let's go back to our mother yeast. Thanks to its technical characteristics and the long leavening it allows to achieve, it is also used to prepare desserts, called large leavened products, such as panettone, pandoro, and colomba.

In fact, for the preparation of these delicacies, neither the use of brewer's yeast nor chemical yeast is recommended. It's not a secret anymore that leavening using brewer's yeast is more manageable due to more reliable and replicable times. Still, despite this, even the large companies use sourdough to produce large leavened products! Have you ever checked the ingredient labels?

But above all, why? What is it that makes mother yeast so unique?

First of all, the shelf life of the products - that is, the time that elapses between the production and consumption of the food without there being any risk to the consumer's health - is much longer if it is natural leavening than with brewer's yeast. Do you remember what I said a moment ago regarding the production of bread with mother yeast, dating back to more than 2000 years ago? This durability over time is due to the type of bacteria present in natural leavening, capable of retaining water, making the product softer, and keeping its freshness longer. This feature allows large factories to produce panettone and pandoro months before their consumption.

Another indisputable reason includes undoubtedly the taste, flavors, and aromas, characteristic of naturally leavened products, which cannot be replicated if brewer's or chemical yeast is used.

Have you ever tried to smell a loaf made with brewer's yeast? It has nothing to do with sourdough bread; there is really no comparison. The same thing goes for the taste. If you have purchased this book, this is probably no secret to you. If you have your own mother yeast, you will know all its virtues, and you will have already benefited from the satisfaction that this leavening can give, and surely you will have prepared bread and pizzas to be envied.

Don't you have your own sourdough starter yet? Well, you can create one!

N.B. The recipes you'll find in this book are based on this starter, with 50% of hydration, but don't worry: you can always convert any recipe to the starter with 100% hydration!

As a gift, with the upper link, you will also get a few savory recipes from my previous books!

Speaking with other sourdough fans, I realized that wild yeast is rarely used for preparing sweet products, such as cakes, brioches, croissants, babà, pancakes and much more, because these delights are often associated with difficult recipes or, perhaps even worse, the use of baking powder.

For this reason, I have created this collection of unique recipes to prepare confectionery products for all tastes... with long leavening!

Personally, for several years I have not thrown a single gram of surplus mother yeast during refreshments! I have so many products that I want to try, both sweet and savory, that it seems that yeast is never enough!

But no more chatter, your sourdough is quivering! I feel it!

Chapter 2

Reminder and useful tips

Rising times and times

If you are a mother yeast fan, the concepts regarding timing and rising times, will probably already be clear to you, so there is a good chance that you are already at an advanced level of leavening knowledge.

However, I would like to look at some concepts together, to remove any doubts and possible uncertainties.

Suppose you have been hanging out in the fantastic world of natural leavening for some time. In that case, you will have already understood that the leavening times are indicative, plus they must be wedged with all the daily commitments, so slow leavening must be learned to be managed. You want to have two virtues: patience and organization.

Several factors influence rising times. These factors are mainly the ambient temperature, humidity, the kneading method, the yeast strength, the flour type, and the total amount of fat included in the recipe.

For this reason, the rising times that you will find in the recipes in this book may vary. However, remember that the element that most affects the rising time is the room temperature.

I do not recommend exceeding 28°C (82°F) during leavening because you could irreversibly damage the bacteria that make up the mother yeast. The optimal leavening temperature has a range between 20°C (68°F) and 25°C. (77°F). Below 20°C (68°F), the mass could have a hard time rising. Often, we will use the fridge, bringing the dough to reach an optimal maturation. Obviously, this does not have the purpose of making the dough rise, but to give new aromas and greater digestibility of the finished product, through the decomposition of complex structures, such as proteins, starches, and fats, into simpler elements. Because of these countless variables, I have not written for each recipe, the precise temperature to make each type of dough rise, but I always try to leave it at a temperature of 23°C (73°F).

One way to keep the dough at optimal temperatures for leavening is to use a leavening cell. Suppose this is not an option, and you need to speed up the leavening. In that case, you could get around the problem by placing the dough inside the oven with the light on or with a saucepan full of hot water, being careful to place the dough away from the light, so you don't risk burning. This technique should be accompanied by a temperature check through a food thermometer.

On the other hand, if you want to slow down the rising time (and at the same time reach an optimal maturation of the dough), you can put the dough in the fridge.

Mother yeast management

Another important variable to keep in mind, is the strength of your mother yeast.

Each yeast is different and variable, depending on which and how many bacteria it contains. The more adult and correctly fed a wild yeast is, the stronger and faster it will let your dough leaven, and the less it will encounter the problem of excessive acidity.

Regardless of the strength of your yeast, you will need to make sure you have thoroughly fed it before using it in recipes.

What do I mean?

I will seem exaggerated, but I want to repeat myself: to obtain an excellent product with natural leavening, you need a superb yeast.

Let's look at the steps to take:

• If the last time you refreshed the yeast was more than three days ago, start refreshing the yeast at least 24 hours before you start the recipe, and refresh it at least twice. If it has been fed in the last three days, you can also feed it 6 to 12 hours earlier. Do not throw away any yeast, as you will need a good amount of it for the recipe.

• If after the refreshments the yeast still has some hint of acid, before the last feed, soak your yeast with 8 ounces of water and 1 teaspoon of caster sugar for half an hour, so that the acidic bacteria detach from it.

• Finally, proceed with the regular feed. Set aside the yeast part for the subsequent preparations and leave the yeast for the recipe at room temperature until it has doubled in volume. This is when the yeast has its greatest strength, it will be perfectly refreshed and will not have any hint of acid.

Conversion to LICOLI yeast.

Solid mother yeast is the type of natural yeast that I personally use. This is why recipes you'll find in this book are balanced for the use of this type of yeast.

On the other hand, if you want to use liquid sourdough (LI.CO.LI), you are free to do so without any problem! I'll show you how.

Use the following conversions:

LI.CO.LI amount = Weight of solid wild yeast / (3 x 2) = weight of liquid natural yeast

I'll give you an example: the recipe says you need 150 g of sourdough. How much LI.CO.LI will you have to use?

LI.CO.LI = 150 / 1.5 = 100 g LI.CO.LI.

* Because LI.CO.LI. is liquid, remember to add a weight equivalent to half the importance of the sourdough (required by the recipe) in flour.

So, if the recipe calls for 150 g of sourdough you will need to put 100 of LI.CO.LI and add the equivalent of half the weight of the required sourdough (150/2) of flour, then 75 g of flour.

This is because of LI.CO.LI is liquid, so you have to compensate for the recipe with more flour!

The dough

The recipes you'll find in this book can be mixed both by hand and by the planetary mixer.

Kneading by hand will take much longer than using a mixer, but it is not impossible (unless you want to make a hand-kneaded DOC panettone at all costs, in that case, you are looking for tough times!).

If you want to proceed with kneading by hand, you will have to work the dough longer and several times during the day. First of all, you will have to create a homogeneous dough, and then you will have to make stops and reinforcements through folds every 1 to 2 hours until it has become homogeneous, smooth, soft, and elastic, and will not stick to the work surface or the bowl.

Using a mixer is much simpler, and the "dough point" (aka when the gluten has been strengthened, necessary in the case of large leavened products) can be achieved with less effort.

One of the pros of using the planetary mixer is that it allows you to play even on higher levels of hydration of the dough, making the final product even softer.

The mistake to avoid is overdoing the kneading to prevent overheating the dough or breaking the gluten mesh.

For the creation of long leavened products, you will have to knead the dough by turning the hook of the planetary mixer for 5, 10, or more minutes to create a dense and strong gluten mesh, which, thanks to the high-fat content, will be able to support the dough during the long leavening.

In the case of long kneading by the planetary mixer, I recommend that you keep the dough temperature under control, which must never exceed 26°C or 78.8°F. In this case, place the dough in the fridge to cool for half an hour. Remember that temperature is one of the key factors in leavening!

Not all recipes provide it, but if you want to make long leavening products, perhaps even with double dough, as is generally done with panettone and pandoro, you need to reach the famous "dough point". To be sure you have reached it, take a piece of dough and try to roll it out with your fingers. If you can form a thin, elastic (and almost transparent!) layer of dough without breaking it, it means that your dough is strung correctly.

It is practically impossible to reach the "dough point" in a highly hydrated dough due to the big amount of liquid. In creating products with high hydration, products with leavening developed more in width than in height will be used.

In this case, I advise you to strengthen these doughs with reinforcement folds, which are different from the classic reinforcement folds for medium hydration doughs.

A highly hydrated dough can be strengthened more efficiently in a bowl. I recommend that you proceed by bringing the dough from the outside to the inside of the mass with the help of a spoon while at the same time turning the bowl. This dough reinforcement procedure should include 2 or 3 turns of folds, one every 15-20 minutes.

I personally prefer to do these 2 to 3 times within an hour - a set of reinforcements every 20 minutes. It leads to a more compact, stronger dough, suitable for a long leavening, with a consequent better maturation.

Ingredients

Types of flour

I won't get you bored with the types of flour to use (I already mentioned this topic in the previous book titled "Authentic Italian Pizza", but I just want to remind you that flours are important, both their quality and their strength, W.

Fortunately, most brands are now starting to include the parameter W in their characteristics as well. In general, all-purpose flour (aka plain flour) or wholemeal flour should never be used alone to create long leavened products, simply because they do not have high strength and tend to create a fragile gluten mesh that breaks after a few hours of leavening.

Another essential thing to consider is that flours with high W value will require many hours of maturation (even 48 to 72 at times), therefore the use of the fridge for the optimal success of the recipe is crucial.

In the recipes that you will find on the following pages, I have not indicated the W of the flour, but I have indicated the type of flour to simplify everything.

I have called the weaker flours "plain flour", those with medium strength, bread flour (also called strong flour), while the strong bread flour (aka very strong flour), has the higher W value. The following table could be used to roughly understand the strength of the flour:

Weaker flour	Strength (W)	Proteins (%)	
	90–130	9–10.5	Plain flour
	130–200	10–11	
	17–200	10.5–11.5	Bread flour
	220–240	12–12.5	
	300–310	13	
Stronger flour	340–400	13.5–15	Strong bread flour

Vanilla types

There are many types of vanilla flavors on the market, including vanilla extract, vanilla essence, vanilla beans, vanillin, and others.

The most natural types, i.e. coming directly from the plant, are vanilla extract and vanilla beans. The vanilla essence, vanillin, and others are chemical products often used in the kitchen, thanks to their affordable cost.

I prefer to use vanilla beans, which are healthier and natural, giving the desserts a fantastic and unmistakable aroma. Obviously, the price of the vanilla beans is quite high, but nobody forbids you to use only a part of it for each preparation. I advise you to use the beans, soaking them in milk (even better if warm milk), or in the sugar, which will acquire its fantastic aroma.

Obviously, choose the type of vanilla aroma that suits you, but keep in mind that, in addition to giving your creation a pleasant aroma, it will serve to cover the hint of egg in the dessert you are going to make.

Sugar quantities

The total amount of sugar in this book's recipes may not be enough for lovers of unbridled sweet desserts!

Having the opportunity to travel, I learned that even in every single World's region, the recipes differ according to the amount of sugar!

So, once you understand what standard my recipes are, you can increase the amount of sugar in the preparation to your liking!

Sparingly, I recommend it!

If you like very sugary sweets, you might increase the sugar by 10%.

Chapter 3

The custards

Vanilla Pastry Cream

Ingredients

- 50 g of caster sugar
- 10 g of plain flour
- 10 g of corn starch
- 200 ml of whole milk
- 2 egg yolks
- ½ vanilla pod
- Orange peel

Directions

- Bring the milk to a boil, then add the orange zest and vanilla;
- Meanwhile, in another saucepan, beat the egg yolks with the caster sugar, add the sifted flour and mix everything with a wooden spoon;
- Pour the hot milk over it a little at a time, continuing to mix with a whisk so as not to leave lumps;
- Put the saucepan on the stove and continue stirring until the cream has thickened;
- Cool the custard in a bowl covered with cling film to make sure no skin forms.

Chocolate Pastry Cream

Ingredients

- 300 g of vanilla pastry cream
- 80 g of dark chocolate

Directions

- Follow the previous recipe for the preparation of vanilla custard (see above);
- Once the custard has thickened, turn off the heat, add the chocolate and stir until it has melted

Vanilla custard Chantilly

Ingredients

- 300 g of vanilla pastry cream
- 180 ml of fresh cream
- 20 g of powdered sugar

Directions

- Follow the recipe for the preparation of vanilla custard (see above);
- With the help of an electric whisk, whip the cream with the powered sugar;
- Once the custard has cooled, add the cream, stirring gently with a spoon from bottom to top, trying not to dismantle the mixture.

Hazelnut chocolate custard

Ingredients

- 100 g of hazelnuts
- 160 g of 85% dark chocolate
- 60 ml of whole or almond milk

Directions

- Toast the hazelnuts in a pan for 5 minutes, once cooled, blend them until you get a compact paste;
- Melt the dark chocolate in a bain-marie or in the microwave, being careful not to burn it;
- Heat the milk, mix it with the dark chocolate and the hazelnut paste, to create a homogeneous cream.

Pistachio and white chocolate custard

Ingredients

- 120 g of shelled pistachios (unsalted)
- 120 g of powdered sugar
- 100 g of white chocolate
- 50 ml of milk
- 30 g of butter

Directions

- Blend the pistachios with the powdered sugar until you get a creamy mixture;
- In a saucepan over low heat, melt the butter and white chocolate. Next, slowly pour in the room temperature milk while constantly stirring;
- Add the pistachio cream, continuing to mix until a homogeneous cream is obtained.

Fruit jam (strawberries)

(You can also use other fruit)

Ingredients

- 300 g of strawberries (frozen too)
- 120 g of caster sugar
- 1/2 apple - Optional (used to accelerate thickening)

Directions

- If you have fresh fruit available, peel it and cut it into small pieces; if you use the frozen one instead, let it defrost at room temperature (or defrost it in the microwave);
- Peel the apple and cut it into small pieces;
- Place a non-stick saucepan on low heat and cook the fruit for 3 minutes covered with the lid;
- Add the caster sugar and continue to cook for about fifteen minutes or until the jam has reached the right consistency (mix the jam frequently so that it does not burn on the bottom);
- Remember that it will tend to solidify a bit once it has cooled, so stop cooking when the jam still feels a little runny compared to the final product you would like; otherwise, you will get a sticky consistency.

Sugar glaze

Ingredients

- 250 g of powdered sugar
- 2 medium egg whites
- Lemon juice

The right proportion between sugar and egg white must be about 125 g of powdered for each egg white of about 30 g.

Directions

- In a bowl, beat 2 egg whites vigorously with a fork until they are lightly foamy (be careful, you don't have to whip it until stiff);
- Sift 250 g of powdered sugar and begin to incorporate the sugar into the egg whites a little at a time, mixing with a spatula from the bottom to top;
- Work the glaze vigorously for 10 minutes until the batter is thick and smooth.
- Add a few drops of lemon and finish mixing;
- At this point, you have reached the royal icing, to which if you want, you can add the food coloring;

If you want to prepare the water-based version of the sugar glaze, it is very simple:

- After sifting the powdered sugar, add a little water a teaspoon at a time, continuing to mix with a spoon until you find a fluid consistency. If you will be using the icing for writing, you will have to prepare it a little harder consistency.

Chapter 4

Laminated doughs

How to make the lamination

I do not deny that making the lamination is not easy, and to be honest, the combo lamination + mother yeast makes this step even more complicated. I assure you that once you succeed, you will not be able to help but prepare croissants, buns and a thousand other goodies at least once a week!

The butter

Let's start with the ingredients, or rather, the main ingredient of the pastry, the butter. The butter must have a very high quality, but it will not be enough to go to the shop and buy the most expensive. The best butter is Bavarian or French butter.

Generally, European-style butter is perfect for laminating dough because it has a much higher fat content (~97% vs ~80% in American-style butter), as well as it tends to have a stronger savory flavor. The higher water content in American butter will steam when baking, creating puffs in the layers.

If you want to dive into the subject, you may have never noticed there are two types of butter: centrifuge and "surfacing" butter (aka the classic butter). They differ by the way of creation. For making the lamination, it is practically obligatory to opt for the centrifuge butter. Why? Well, an old cheesemaker friend confided to me that the production of cheeses collects all the best parts of the milk, especially in Italy. And it is for this reason, the cheapest types of butter are those obtained with the surfacing method, which is produced during a phase of cheese or other dairy productions. For this reason, I suggest you, at least for the preparation of laminated dough, use butter obtained from a centrifuge such as the Bavarian one.

The centrifuge butter has the right technical qualities and the right plasticity, which interests us in preparing quality laminated products. Why is plasticity so important?

Well, I am sure you won't ruin hours of work because of the butter! If the butter is not plastic, it is possible that, during the folding, the layers of butter between one sheet and the other have crystallized and begin to break and mix with the rest of the dough, ruining all work done.

Think about it, in laminated dough products, the butter is used to interpose itself between one layer of dough and the other, making sure that they do not mix with each other (during the lamination, the dough needs to be folded several times on itself, creating even more than 100 puff pastry...if needed!).

As you can see, our main goal is to keep the layers of butter as intact as possible.

Have you already tried to make laminated products, but after cooking, did you realize that the product is not at all flaky, but only leavened like a brioche?

I'll come with some advice!

First of all, grab some professional margarine suitable specifically for lamination. Use the same amount provided for the butter in the recipes. You will see that it will be something else entirely! Obviously, the lamination will be easier to obtain, and the taste will be less buttery. If you are a butter lover however, you could add a small part of butter to the dough (if it does not already include it, you can add 5-10% of butter of the weight of the flour).

On the other hand, if you would like to approach the original French recipe in which only butter is present, you could make the butter more plastic by mixing it with flour before its use, thus avoiding the famous breakages during the folding phases. How much flour to use? I would say not to use more than 10% of the weight of the butter needed for the lamination. For example, if the recipe calls for 200 g of butter, you will need to create a plastic dough consisting of 200 g of butter and no more than 20 g of flour. If you have a planetary mixer, it will make your job easier.

The temperature

In addition to the butter quality, another variable to take into account for creating the perfect lamination is the dough temperature, or rather the butter temperature.

The greatest difficulty in preparing a peeled and leavened product lies in finding the right operating temperature.

While for the preparation of the lamination, we have to take care to keep the dough at a cold temperature so as not to melt the butter, in the leavened dough, we have to deal with the needs of the mother yeast, which must stay warm in order to let the dough rise. Since the mother yeast allows a slower leavening than the brewer's yeast does, dealing with laminated natural yeast dough has a triple difficulty, namely the long leavening times.

Keep in mind that the butter at 25/ 28°C (77/82.4°F) begins to melt and mix with the rest of the dough (with the consequence that the lamination being cooked will lower down, instead of rising). Meanwhile, the mother yeast should be kept at 25°C/77°F to allow optimal leavening.

That said, I found that the best solution is to let the laminated dough rise at a temperature between 20 and 25°C (68/77°F). In addition, if the dough has already been doubled in volume before starting the lamination process, it should be active to perform another volume doubling in a short time.

The flour

Flour is often one of those ingredients that gets "snubbed" a little. Yet it is also essential, especially for creating puff pastry with mother yeast. The dough will have to withstand a long leavening of more than 8 hours and must not let the butter escape between the lamination.

If you choose a flour with low strength (low W), the dough will not stand the leavening, and the gluten mesh will tend to pierce, compromising the final result. I tend to use flours for large leavened products with W around 350. If your sourdough still doesn't have the strength to rise with very strong flours, you could opt for a W of 300, but don't go below 270.

Getting the butter ready

lato interno10 cm circa

First, take a sheet of baking paper, divide it as in the picture, and put the stick of butter in the area I highlighted in white

 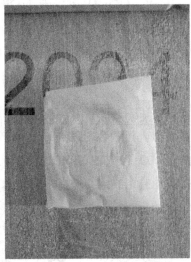 

Close the side flaps on the dough and then the ones above and below.

Turn over the dough embedded in the baker paper and start pressing the butter well on all sides to make it take the square shape.

Press well even at the vertices.
Put the butter thus created in the fridge until the dough is ready, and you can start making the lamination.

The dough lamination
The total time for dough lamination is about two and a half hours (30 minutes of rest in the fridge between one set and the next, plus the

time dedicated to laminating). This is a total of 3 sets of folds. My favorite method is to make two sets of three folds (folding the dough in 3) and a series of 4 folds (folding the dough in 4). The total number of thresholds is thus (3 x 3 x 4 =) 36 sheets.
Are you ready? Let's go!

 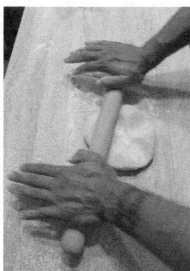 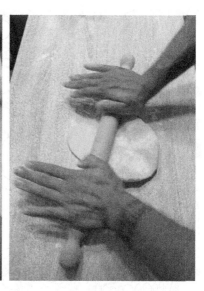

Take the leavened dough out of the fridge and, with the help of the rolling pin, press it forming a cross, dividing it into 4.

Start rolling out one wedge at a time.

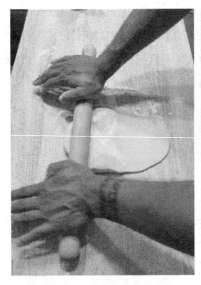

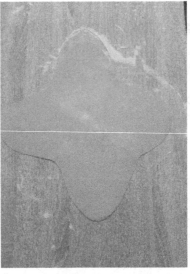

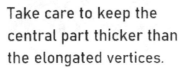

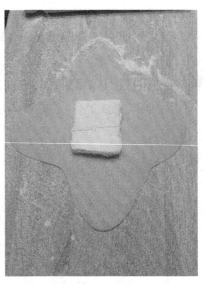

Then proceed with the opposite one.

And finally, move on to the other two.

Take care to keep the central part thicker than the elongated vertices.

Take the butter (that we made in the previous section) out of the fridge, unwrap and place in the center of the cross.

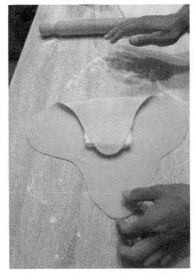

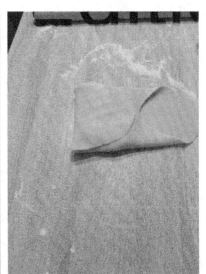

Wrap the shaped butter with the dough, as shown in the photo.

Once the dough is completely wrapped, check that it is tightly closed on all sides. The butter must have no escape routes. Turn the dough with the edges towards the base.

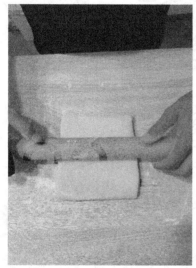 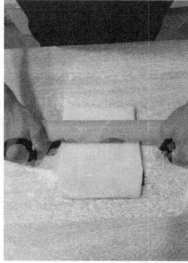 

Start gently pressing the dough filled with the butter with the help of the rolling pin. You press it, move and press again, along the entire length, about ten times

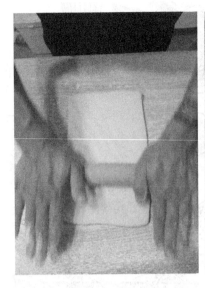  

Once this is done, begin to roll out the dough with a rolling pin until you get the length, as in the photo. Use flour to keep the dough from sticking to the work surface and the rolling pin.

You have come to the first set of folds:

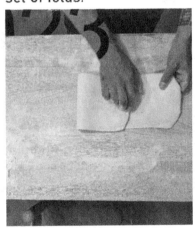  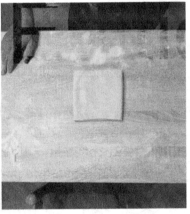

Fold 1/3 of the dough towards the center.

Fold the other vertex of the dough towards the center.

Cover the transparent dough with cling film.

Refrigerate for 30 minutes, so that the butter and the dough are again at the ideal and same temperature, preventing the butter from melting during the subsequent processing.

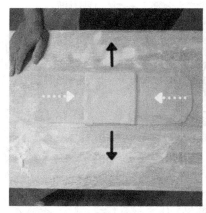  

Take the dough out of the fridge and place it with the 3 folds facing you. In the previous step, you folded in the direction of the yellow arrows, now you will have to fold in the direction of the black arrows.

Here is a detail of the direction of rolling out. Start to roll out, initially you helping with the pressure of the rolling pin and then rolling it out in the traditional way. The fold is 90 degrees compared to the first set.

And thus begins the second set of three-folds.

Fold the other vertex of the strip toward the center.

Fold the other vertex of the strip toward the center.

Cover the dough with cling film and refrigerate for 30 minutes.

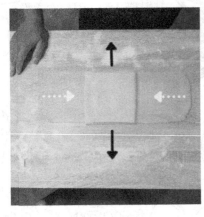

You will find yourself in this situation once again. Check the direction in which you made the last set of folds and stretch in the opposite direction!

In this direction!

Help yourself with light pressure on the dough.

And then roll it out with a rolling pin.

Now make the last set of 4 folds.

Fold one end of the pastry until it reaches the center.

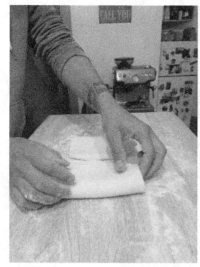 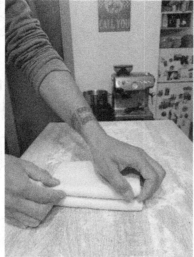 

And then fold the other end up to the center.

Fold the already folded dough in two like this.

Put your dough in the fridge for at least half an hour and it will be ready to be used!

4.1 – Italian pan au chocolat

Ingredients

- 150 g of mother yeast
- 400 g of strong (or bread) flour
- 60 g of caster sugar
- 50 g of butter at room temperature
- 175 ml of water
- 2 teaspoons of salt
- 150 g of chocolate chips for the filling
- 20 ml of milk for brushing
- Powdered sugar for sprinkling
- 180 g of butter for peeling

To complete:

- 1 beaten egg + vanilla
- Vanilla or chocolate custard

Directions

- Dissolve 150 g of mother yeast in 175 ml of water;
- Add 400 g of previously sifted strong flour, 60 g of caster sugar, yeast dissolved in water to the mixer a little at a time and start kneading with the leaf at medium speed;
- Also add 2 teaspoons of salt and 50 g of soft butter cut into small pieces and continue to knead;

- When all the ingredients have gathered around the leaf hook, replace the leaf with the hook and knead for 10 minutes on medium speed;
- After 10 minutes, and when the dough comes off the walls well and remains attached to the hook, move the dough onto a lightly floured pastry board. Work it with your hands and create a rectangular dough; wrap it in plastic wrap and let it rest at room temperature for at least 2 hours;
- After the resting time, put the dough in the fridge for an hour;
- In the meantime, prepare the stick of butter for peeling: give it the shape, following the steps at the beginning of the chapter, and put it back in the fridge for another half hour;
- When the butter has cooled down again, take out both the butter and the dough. Time for the lamination! You can follow the steps described in the previous pages;
- Once the dough has been laminated and spent the last 30 minutes in the fridge, you are ready to prepare the pan au chocolat! Roll out the dough on a floured pastry board until you get a rectangle of 25x40 cm / 9 x15.5", with a thickness of around 3-4 mm / 0.15";
- Cut the rectangle obtained in two equal parts along the length so as to have two rectangles with the dimensions of about 12x40 cm / 5x15", then cut the two rectangles into 5 parts, obtaining rectangles of 8x12 cm / 3x5";
- At this point, distribute a teaspoon of chocolate chips on the 8 cm / 3" side and roll the pastry over them only once, distribute another teaspoon of chocolate chips and finish rolling the dough;
- Place them on a baking sheet lined with baking paper, placing the closure of the pastry under the bun, otherwise it will tend to lose its initial shape!
- Cover the pan with cling film and let it rise at a temperature that does not exceed 23-25 °C/77°F for about 6/8 hours until doubled;
- Turn on the oven in static mode and bring it to 200°C/390°F;

- Brush the surface of the saccottini with beaten egg with vanilla and bake them for about 20 minutes, until golden brown;
- Before serving, sprinkle them with powdered sugar;
- You can enjoy your empty croissants, or fill them with jam, or vanilla, or chocolate custard. Check out the recipes in Chapter 2 to understand how to make them!
- If the croissant has risen correctly, there should be enough space for the filling (with a pastry bag insert the cream in two places). Otherwise, you can cut the croissant in half and stuff it like this.

4.2 – The spelled and kefir croissant

Ingredients

- 180 g of mother yeast
- 350 g of spelled flour
- 100 g of strong (bread) flour
- 100 ml of kefir or yogurt
- 2 eggs
- 1 tablespoon of caster sugar
- 1 pinch of salt
- 1 vanilla bean
- 200 g of butter for laminating
  Topping:
- 25 ml of water
- 40 g of caster sugar
- 10 g of honey
- Vanilla or chocolate custard

Directions

- Dissolve 180 g of mother yeast in 100 ml of kefir (or yogurt) in the bowl of the mixer using the whisk;
- Add 100 g of strong flour, continuing to mix with the leaf;
- At this point, add 2 eggs, 1 tablespoon of caster sugar, a pinch of salt, and the vanilla;

- When the dough is homogeneous, add the 350 g of spelled flour in 3 parts and when the dough begins to be more compact, replace the leaf with the hook and knead until a homogeneous and strung dough is obtained;
- As the dough comes off the walls well and remains attached to the hook, move the dough onto a lightly floured pastry board and let it rest for 10 minutes covered with a cloth;
- Work the dough with your hands and create a rectangular dough; put it in a hermetically sealed container and let it rise for 6/8 hours or until doubled;
- Once doubled, put it in the fridge for at least 2 hours to make it ready for peeling: butter and dough must have the same temperature;
- In the meantime, prepare the stick of butter for the lamination: give it the shape, following the steps at the beginning of the chapter, and put it back in the fridge for another half hour;
- When the butter has cooled down, take out both the butter and the dough. We have reached the moment of lamination; you can follow the steps described in the previous pages. I generally start making the folds of the pastry in the late afternoon to perform the last leavening during the night;
- Now that the pastry is done, we need to give shape to the croissants:
- Roll out the dough with the help of a rolling pin to create a 25x40 cm / 9 x15" rectangle; the dough must have a thickness of 3 mm maximum;
- Use a very sharp knife to form the triangles: suppose you are looking at the dough with the longest side placed horizontally: you will create triangles of 8 cm base x 25 cm in height / 3x9" (you should get 10 triangles);
- Make a 1.5 cm /0.6" cut in the center of the base of the triangle perpendicular to it, and form the croissants by rolling the sheet on itself starting from the base up to the

tip (the cut at the base serves to widen the triangle a little more to give it the curved shape);

- Then finish rolling and place the tip of the pastry under the croissant so that it maintains its shape both during leavening and cooking;
- Place the formed croissants on a baking tray lined with parchment paper, and cover them with cling film, leaving them to rise for about 6-8 hours at a maximum temperature of 23-25 °C / 73-77 °F until doubled in volume;
- Bake in a convection oven at 170°C / 338°F for about fifteen minutes or until they have a nice golden color;
- Bring a solution made of 25 ml of water, 40 g of caster sugar, and 10 g of honey to a boil and let it cook for about a minute, making sure it does not burn; once cold, pour it over the croissants that are still hot to make them shiny;
- You can enjoy your empty croissants or fill them with jam, vanilla, or chocolate custard. Check out the recipes in Chapter 3 to follow the recipes!
- If the croissant has risen correctly, there should be enough space for the filling (with a pastry bag, insert the cream in two places). Otherwise, you can cut the croissant in half and stuff it.

4.3 – The bicolor croissant

Ingredients

Light dough

- 130 g of mother yeast
- 275 g of very strong (or strong bread) flour
- 70 g of caster sugar
- 100 ml of water
- 1 pinch of salt
- 140 g of butter for puff pastry

Dark dough

- 40 g of mother yeast
- 100 g of very strong (or strong bread) flour
- 50 g of caster sugar
- 40 ml of water
- 25 g of unsweetened cocoa powder
- 1 pinch of salt

Topping

- 1 beaten egg + milk and vanilla
- Vanilla or chocolate custard

Directions
Light dough

- In the bowl of the mixer, dissolve 130 g of yeast with 100 ml of water;
- Replace the whisk with the leaf and combine 70 g of caster sugar, and 275 g of flour a little at a time;
- Replace the leaf with the hook and knead until a homogeneous and strung dough is obtained;
- Once the dough comes off the walls well and remains attached to the hook, move the dough onto a lightly floured pastry board and let it rest for 10 minutes;

Dark dough

- Dissolve 40 g of yeast in 40 ml of water, then add 50 g of sugar, and continue to mix with the leaf gradually adding 100 g of flour, previously mixed with 25 g of unsweetened cocoa and a pinch of salt;
- Continue with the hook, and once the dough comes off the walls, move it to a lightly floured pastry board and let it rest for 10 minutes.

Both doughs

- Work the dough with your hands, creating two rectangular loaves; put them in two hermetically sealed containers and let them rise for 6/8 hours or until doubled (if you want to opt for a longer leavening, let it rise at room temperature for 3 hours and then 12 hours in the fridge);
- Once doubled, put them in the fridge for at least 2 hours, in order to make them ready for peeling (butter and dough must have the same temperature);
- In the meantime, prepare the stick of butter for laminating: give it the shape, following the steps at the beginning of the chapter, and put it back in the fridge for another half hour;

- When the butter has cooled down take out both the butter and the dough. It is time to laminate! You can follow the steps described in the previous pages, but do them only for the yellow dough;
- Once the puff pastry is obtained, you need to shape the croissants!
- Roll out both the yellow puffed dough and the black dough with a rolling pin until it reaches a size of about 20 x 20 cm / 8x8".
- Lay the black dough on the yellow and continue rolling them together with a rolling pin to form a two-colored rectangle measuring 25 x 40 cm / 9x15", with a thickness of 2 - 3mm / 0.1";
- With a sharp knife, cut the pastry to obtain triangles of 8 cm of base x 25 cm of height /3x9" (you should get 10 triangles);
- Make a 1.5 /0.6" cm cut in the center of the base of the triangle perpendicular to it, and form the croissants by rolling the sheet on itself starting from the base up to the tip;
- Then finish rolling and place the tip of the pastry under the croissant so that it maintains its shape both during leavening and cooking;
- Place the formed croissants on a baking sheet lined with parchment paper, and cover them with cling film, letting them rise at a maximum temperature of 23-25°C / 73-77°F for about 6-8 hours until doubled in volume;
- Beat an egg with 1 tablespoon of milk and a little vanilla and brush it on the croissants before baking;
- Cook in a convection oven, with a pan of water inside at 170°C / 338°F for about 15-20 minutes until they have a nice golden color.

You can enjoy your plain croissants or fill them with jam, or vanilla or chocolate custard. Check out Chapter 3 to find filling recipes!
If the croissant has risen correctly, there should be enough space for the filling (with a pastry bag, insert the cream in two places). Otherwise, you can cut the croissant in half and fill it!

4.4 – The pan au chocolat

Ingredients

- 100 g of mother yeast
- 250 g of strong (or bread) flour
- 150 g almond milk
- 110 g butter (for puff pastry)
- 1 drop of vanillin
- A pinch of salt
- 60 g of caster sugar
- 50 g of dark chocolate (possibly 14 strips of 8 cm /3", otherwise the chocolate chips will be fine)

Directions

- Dissolve 100 g of mother yeast in 150 ml of almond milk at room temperature, using a whisk;
- If you use the planetary mixer with a leaf hook, add 120 g of flour, and then slowly add the other ingredients: 60 g of caster sugar, a pinch of salt, and vanillin. When the dough is homogeneous, add the other 125 g of flour. When the dough starts to be more compact, replace the leaf with the hook and knead until you get a homogeneous dough: once the dough comes off well from the walls and remains attached to the

hook, move the dough on a pastry board lightly floured and leave to rest for 10 minutes;

- Work the dough with your hands and create a rectangular dough; put it in an airtight container and let it rise for 2 hours out of the fridge and then put it in the fridge for another 12 hours;
- Take it out of the fridge and let it rise until doubled: it will take about 4/5 hours. Once doubled in volume, put it in the fridge for at least 30 minutes in order to make it ready for laminating: butter and dough must have the same temperature.
- In the meantime, prepare the stick of butter for lamination: give it the shape, following the steps at the beginning of the chapter, and put it back in the fridge for another half hour;
- When the butter has cooled down take out both the butter and the dough. We have reached the moment of leafing; you can follow the steps described in the previous pages. Now that the dough is ready let's shape the pan au chocolat!
- Create a 25 x 56 cm / 9x21" rectangle with the help of a rolling pin; the dough must have a thickness of 2/3 mm / 0.1" maximum;
- With a very sharp knife, cut 7 rectangles of 8 cm x 25 cm / 3x9" in height.
- Place a chocolate stick parallel to the shorter side, and start rolling the dough around it; when there are 10 cm / 4" left to complete the rolling, put another rod and close the cylinder; remember to position the closure below in order to avoid losing its shape, during leavening and cooking;
- Place the formed pan au chocolat on a baking tray lined with parchment paper, and cover them with cling film, letting them rise for about 6 hours or until doubled in volume;
- Bake at 180°C / 356°F for about 25 minutes;
- Bring a solution made of 25 ml of water, 40 g of caster sugar, and 10 g of honey to a boil and let it cook for about a minute, making sure it does not burn; once cold, pour it over the croissants that are still hot to make them shiny.

4.5 – The white chocolate croissant

Ingredients

- 100 g of mother yeast
- 240 g of very strong (or strong bread) flour
- 50 g of caster sugar
- 60 ml of water
- 65 g of white chocolate
- 15 g of butter
- 1 egg
- 1 pinch of salt

Topping:
- beaten egg + milk and vanilla
- Vanilla or chocolate custard

Directions

- Slice 65 g of white chocolate into flakes, place It In a container in a bain-marie with 15 g of butter, let them melt, and then bring them to room temperature;
- Dissolve 100 g of mother yeast in 60 ml of water with 50 g of caster sugar;
- Add 1 egg and a pinch of salt to the mixture and continue mixing;

- Once the butter and chocolate mixture is at room temperature, add it to the yeast mixture and mix to make it homogeneous;
- Knead, adding 240 g of flour a little at a time, to create a smooth and strung dough;
- Let it rest for 2 hours at room temperature in an airtight container, then place it in the fridge for about 12 hours to rise;
- In the meantime, prepare the stick of butter for laminating: give it the shape, following the steps at the beginning of the chapter, and put it back in the fridge for another half hour;
- When the butter has cooled down, take out both the butter and the dough. Lamination time! You can follow the steps described in the previous pages. I generally start making the folds of the pastry in the late afternoon in order to let it leaven during the night;
- Once the puff pastry is obtained, you can shape white chocolate croissants!
- Create a rectangle 32 x 25 cm / 12x9" with the help of a rolling pin (the dough must have a thickness of 4 mm maximum);
- With a sharp knife, cut the pastry in triangles of 8 cm of base x 25 cm / 3x9" of height (you should get 8 triangles);
- Make a 1.5 cm / 0.6"cut in the center of the base of the triangle perpendicular to it, and form the croissants by rolling the sheet on itself starting from the base up to the tip;
- Place the tip of the pastry under the croissant so that it maintains its shape both during leavening and cooking;
- Place the formed croissants on a baking tray lined with parchment paper, and cover them with cling film, leaving them to rise for about 6-8 hours at a maximum temperature of 23-25°C / 73-77°F until doubled in volume;
- Beat an egg with 1 tablespoon of milk and a little vanilla and brush it on the croissants before baking;
- Cook the white chocolate croissants in a convection oven, with a saucepan of water inside at 170°C / 338°F for about 15-20 minutes until they have a nice golden color.

You can enjoy your plain croissants or fill them with jam, or vanilla or chocolate custard. Check out the recipes in Chapter 3! If the croissant has risen correctly, there should be enough space for the filling (with a pastry bag, insert the cream in two places), otherwise, you can cut the croissant in half and fill it.

4.6 – The Croissant - French recipe

Ingredients

- 100 g of mother yeast
- 340 g of very strong (or strong bread) flour
- 50 g of butter
- 30 g of caster sugar
- 80 ml of cold water
- 60 ml of cold milk
- 1 teaspoon of honey
- 5 g of salt
- 165 g of butter for peeling

To top:

- 1 beaten egg + milk and vanilla
- Vanilla or chocolate custard

Directions

- In the planetary mixer, dissolve 100 grams of wild yeast in a mixture of 80 ml of water, 60 ml of milk, 1 teaspoon of honey, and 30 g of caster sugar with the help of the whisk;
- Add half the flour (170 g) a little at a time and continue mixing;
- Replace the whisk with the leaf and continue to knead, also adding the other half of the flour (170 g);

- Add 50 g of soft butter cut into small pieces and knead for about 10 minutes, at a moderate speed;
- Once the dough is firm, strung and not sticky, turn off the planetary mixer, place it in a container with a lid and let it rise at room temperature for about 12 hours, or until it doubles.
- Put the dough in the fridge for about an hour to bring it to the same temperature as the butter;
- In the meantime, prepare the stick of butter for laminating: give it the shape, following the steps at the beginning of the chapter, and put it back in the fridge for another half hour;
- When the butter has cooled down, take out both the butter and the dough. Now is lamination time. You can follow the steps described in the previous pages. I generally start making the folds in the late afternoon, to allow for the leavening during the night;
- Once you have made the lamination, put the dough in the fridge one last time, in order to relax it and be ready for the subsequent portioning and shaping;
- Create a 40 x 25 cm / 9x15" rectangle with the help of a rolling pin (the dough must have a thickness of 4 mm maximum);
- With a sharp knife, cut the pastry into triangles of 8 cm (base) x 25 cm (height) / 3x9. You should get 10 triangles;
- Make a 1.5 cm cut in the center of the base of the triangle perpendicular to it, and form the croissants by rolling the sheet on itself starting from the base up to the tip;
- Then finish rolling and place the tip of the pastry under the croissant so that it maintains its shape both during leavening and cooking;
- Place the formed croissants on a baking tray lined with parchment paper, and cover them with cling film, leaving them to rise for about 6-8 hours at a maximum temperature of 23-25 °C / 73-77°F until doubled in volume;
- Beat an egg with 1 tablespoon of milk and a little vanilla and brush it on the croissants before baking;
- Bake the French croissants in a pre-heated oven at 200°C / 392°F for about 20 minutes until golden brown.

You can enjoy your plain croissants or fill them with jam, or vanilla, or chocolate custard. Check out the recipes in Chapter 3!
If the croissant has risen correctly, there should be enough space for the filling. With a pastry bag, insert the cream in two places, or you can cut the croissant in half and fill it.

4.7 – The chocolate croissant

Ingredients

- 70 g of mother yeast
- 230 g of very strong (or strong bread) flour
- 75 g of caster sugar
- 70 ml of water
- 40 g of bitter cocoa
- 1 egg
- Vanilla beans
- 1 pinch of salt
- 100 g of butter for laminating

To top:
- Powdered sugar

- Vanilla or chocolate custard

Directions

- In the mixer, dissolve 70 g of yeast in 70 ml of water, then add 75 g of caster sugar;
- Operate the leaf and add half of the very strong (bread) flour (115 g) and when the mixture begins to be homogeneous, add 1 egg, vanilla and a pinch of salt;

- Sift the remaining 115 g of very strong (bread) flour with the bitter cocoa and then add them little by little to the dough;
- Replace the leaf with the hook and continue kneading until the dough is firm and not sticky, place it in an airtight container and let it rest in the fridge for more than 12 hours;
- In the meantime, prepare the stick of butter for lamination: give it the shape, following the steps at the beginning of the chapter, and put it back in the fridge for another half hour;
- When the butter has cooled down, and the dough has rested for at least 12 hours, it is time for peeling. You can follow the steps described in the previous pages;
- Once you have obtained the puff pastry, place it in the fridge one last time for another 30 minutes to relax it and be ready for the subsequent drafting and shaping.
- It's time to make chocolate croissants!
- Roll out the dough with the help of a rolling pin and a little flour to obtain a rectangle of 35x25 cm / 15x9" with a maximum thickness of 4 mm /0.15".
- With a sharp knife, cut rectangles measuring 7 x 25 cm /3x9" and then divide them by their diagonal.
- In the shorter side of the triangle make a small cut of about 1.5 cm / 0.6", perpendicular to the cut, and roll it up to the top.
- Let the croissants rise overnight or until doubled;
- Bake in a pre-heated oven at 170°C / 338°F for about 15/20 minutes until golden brown;
- Once cooked, sprinkle the croissants with powdered sugar.

If the croissant has risen correctly, there should be enough space for the filling. With a pastry bag, insert the cream in two places, or you can cut the croissant in half and fill it.

Chapter 5

Braided doughs

5.1 - The Kringel

Ingredients

- 120 g of mother yeast
- 390 g of strong (or bread) flour
- 120 ml of milk
- 85 g of caster sugar
- 2 eggs
- 30 ml of extra virgin olive oil
- 1 tablespoon of honey
- The zest of ½ lemon and ½ orange
- 1 vanilla bean
- 1 teaspoon of salt

Filling:

- 100 g of butter at room temperature
- 50 g of cane sugar
- 60 g of raisins
- Cinnamon

Directions

- Warm 120 ml of milk, then place it in the bowl of the mixer together with 120 g of yeast, 1 tablespoon of honey, vanilla and start kneading;
- Add 2 eggs, 85 g of caster sugar, 30 ml of extra virgin olive oil, the zest of ½ lemon and ½ orange and continue to knead for a few minutes;
- Add 390 g of flour a little at a time until it is incorporated, finally add 1 teaspoon of salt;
- Continue to knead at low speed for another 5 minutes until the dough is strung;
- Form a ball, place it in an airtight container and let it rise for at least 4/5 hours at room temperature;
- In the meantime, prepare the buttercream, whipping 100 g of butter at around 20°C / 68°F and 50 g of cane sugar with an electric whisk (whip everything for a few minutes until you get a soft cream);
- Roll out the dough with a rolling pin, obtaining a rectangle of about 50 x 35 cm / 20x13.5" and spread the buttercream on it (leaving some aside for the final brushing), 60 g of raisins previously soaked in warm water, and a little cinnamon to taste;
- Roll up the rectangle starting from the longest side, then cut the cylinder obtained in half lengthwise and twist the two halves together, obtaining a braid. Place the crown-shaped braid in a 24 cm /9.5" round baking pan and brush the surface with the rest of the previously prepared buttercream;
- Cover with cling film and leave to rise for about 8 hours at room temperature (not in the oven with the light on, otherwise the butter filling will melt);
- When doubled, bake in a preheated oven at 180°C / 356°F for 40/45 minutes. (If the top tends to cook too quickly, cover it with a sheet of aluminum foil.) Once cooked, let it cool and dry on a rack before serving.

5.2 - The yogurt braid with hazelnuts and chocolate

Ingredients

- 110 g of mother yeast
- 240 + 100 g of strong (or bread) flour
- 75 g of caster sugar
- 20 ml of water
- 125 g of hazelnut yogurt
- 2 eggs
- 50 g of butter at room temperature
- 1 teaspoon of honey
- 1 pinch of salt
- Vanilla beans

Filling - Ingredients:

- 80 gr dark chocolate
- 60 g of hazelnut yogurt
- 1 handful of chopped hazelnuts

Directions

- Dissolve 110 g of sourdough in 20 ml of water, then install the leaf and add half a portion of yogurt (60 g), 240 g of flour and start kneading at medium-low speed;
- When the dough is homogeneous, add the remaining 65 g of yogurt, 75 g of caster sugar, 1 teaspoon of honey, 2 eggs, vanilla, 1 pinch of salt and continue to knead;
- When the mixture begins to blend, add 50 g of soft butter cut into small pieces and continue to knead until it is incorporated;
- After 5 minutes, put on the hook, add another 100 g of flour and continue kneading at moderate speed until the dough is stringed (if you notice that the dough takes too long to string and gets too hot, put it in the fridge for about 15 minutes, after which it will be easier to get to stringing);
- Let the dough rest for an hour outside the fridge, then place it in the fridge in an airtight container for 8 hours or overnight;
- Take out the dough and let it rise until it has more than doubled in volume (it should take about 4 hours);
- In the meantime, melt 80 g of dark chocolate in a bain-marie, and when it has cooled, add it to 60 g of hazelnut yogurt;
- Roll out the dough evenly with the help of a rolling pin, giving it a rectangular shape of about 30 x 50 cm / 12x20";
- Sprinkle some flour on the work surface and place the rectangle of dough on top so that it does not stick in the next step;
- Spread the dark chocolate and yogurt cream evenly over the entire surface of the dough and add a handful of toasted and chopped hazelnuts;
- Now roll the rectangle on itself starting from the longest part, then cut the roll in half lengthwise using a sharp knife;
- Now make the braid with the two half-cylinders, being careful and leave the cut and most beautiful part to be seen towards the outside;
- Place the braid in a plum cake or ring mold in a round pan;
- Let it rise at room temperature until it has more than doubled (about 8 hours), then gently brush the surface with a bit of milk;

- Bake the braid at 180°C / 350 °F in a preheated static oven for about 30/35 minutes, until it is golden brown;
  - Place on a rack to cool and dry.

5.3 - The chocolate-vanilla braid

Ingredients

- 130 g of mother yeast
- 270 g of very strong (or strong bread) flour
- 70 g of caster sugar
- 70 g of butter at room temperature
- 150 + 20 ml of milk
- 1 egg
- 1 tablespoon of honey
- 30 g of bitter cocoa powder
- 1 pinch of salt
- Vanilla beans
- a couple of tablespoons of caster sugar for sprinkling before baking

Directions

- Dissolve 130 g of yeast in 150 ml of milk, 70 g of caster sugar, 1 teaspoon of honey, and vanilla beans;
- Blend the ingredients in the mixer, next add 70 g of soft butter cut into small pieces, 1 egg and a pinch of salt;
- Finally, add 270 g of flour a little at a time until it is completely incorporated into the dough;

- Once the mixture is homogeneous and begins to detach from the walls of the mixer, take the dough and divide it in half;
- Leave half of it in the mixer, add 30 grams of unsweetened cocoa and another 20 ml of milk and turn again until the dough detaches from the mixer again;
- Form each of the two previously prepared doughs into a ball and place them to rest in two airtight containers for about 3 hours at room temperature;
- Divide the two doughs again into 2 equal parts: you will get 4 portions, two of which with cocoa and two with vanilla;
- Roll them out on a surface to obtain four cylinders about 40cm /15.5" long, helping with a little flour in case the dough is too sticky;
- Form a braid and place it in a plum cake mold, or in a ring in a pan;
- Let it rise overnight in the heat (25°C / 75°F), or in the oven with the light on;
- After about 8 hours, or when the braid has doubled in volume, proceed with baking in a convection oven at 160°C / 320°F for about 30 minutes;
- Once the dough is golden brown, the braid will be ready to be taken out of the oven and left to cool on a rack;
- I suggest you serve her this braid with an exquisite Chantilly cream. You can find the recipe for this delicious cream in chapter 3.

5.4 – The bicolor pistachio-vanilla braid

Ingredients

- 110 g of mother yeast
- 310 g of very strong (or strong bread) flour
- 70 g of caster sugar
- 70 g of butter at room temperature
- 1 egg
- 90 ml of milk
- 60 ml of water
- Vanilla beans
- 1 pinch of salt
- 55 g of pistachio spread cream
- 20 g of pistachio flour
- 20 g of chopped pistachios

Directions

- Dissolve 110 g of mother yeast in 90 ml of milk, 60 ml of water, 70 g of caster sugar and vanilla;
- Blend ingredients in the mixer then add 70 g of soft butter into small pieces, 1 egg, and 1 pinch of salt;
- Finally add 310 g of flour a little at a time and continue to spin at medium speed until it is completely incorporated;

- Once the mixture begins to detach from the walls of the mixer, take the dough and divide it in half;
- Leave half of it in the mixer, add 55 g of pistachio cream and 20 g of pistachio flour;
- Keep mixing until the dough detaches itself from the mixer, then form two balls for each of the two doughs and put them to rise overnight at room temperature (23°C/ 70-75°F) in two airtight containers;
- Roll out and stretch each of the two doughs so that they form two elongated cylinders of about 60 cm /23" and form a two-color braid with them;
- Place the braid in a fairly large plum cake mold or in a round pan and let it rise, covered with cling film, until tripled (about 8 hours);
- Decorate the top of the braid with chopped pistachios and bake in a preheated oven at 180°C / 355°F for 30 minutes or until golden brown.
- I suggest you serve this sweet braid with some tasty pistachio cream and white chocolate. You can find the recipe for this delicious cream in chapter 3 "The custards".

5.5 - The chocolate and apricot braid

Ingredients

- 100 g of mother yeast
- 150 g of very strong (or strong bread) flour
- 100 g of almond flour
- 50 g of plain (or all purpose) flour
- 90 g of caster sugar
- 120 ml of milk
- 1 egg
- 50 g of vanilla custard
- 70 g of dark chocolate
- 150 g of apricot jam

Directions

- Dissolve 100 g of mother yeast in 130 ml of milk together with 90 g of caster sugar;
- Add 1 egg and knead at medium speed;
- In the meantime, make a flour mix consisting of 150 g of very strong flour, 100 g of almond flour, and 50 g of all-purpose flour, sifting well;
- Add the flour mix a little at a time in the mixer and turn until stringing;

- Let the dough rest for about 2 hours at room temperature in an airtight container;
- Leave the dough to mature in the fridge for about 8 hours;
- Once the dough has been taken out of the fridge, reinforce it by rolling it several times on itself in all directions, in order to give strength to the gluten mesh;
- Wait about an hour and a half, so that the dough is relaxed and easier to handle;
- In the meantime, Heat 50 ml of cream on low, it comes to a boil, turn off the heat and add 70 g of dark chocolate cut into flakes and mix until it is completely melted;
- Now roll out the dough with a rolling pin with the help of some flour, until you get a fairly thin rectangle of about 15x60 cm / 6x24";
- At this point spread the warmed ganache on the dough evenly and then the apricot jam;
- Roll the dough starting from the longest side, in order to obtain a nice long roll; Cut the roll in half lengthwise with a sharp knife, then weave the two halves together;
- Place the braid in a plum cake pan or ring-shaped in a round pan and let it rise until the dough has tripled in volume (it may take about 4-5 hours);
- Bake in a preheated and ventilated oven at 180°C / 355°F for about 30 minutes or until golden brown;
- Once cooked, let it cool on a rack before serving. I recommend accompanying it with delicious whipped cream!

5.6 – The tricolor braid

Ingredients

- 100 g mother yeast
- 390 g of very strong (or strong bread) flour
- 160 ml of milk
- 250 g of ricotta
- 90 g of caster sugar
- 4 tablespoons pistachio spread cream
- 70 g of white chocolate
- 20 g of unsweetened cocoa powder
- Vanilla beans

Directions

- Start by mixing 100 g of mother yeast, 160 ml of milk, 90 g of caster sugar, 250 g of ricotta, and Vanilla beans until you get a homogeneous mixture without lumps;
- Divide the mixture into 3 equal parts and proceed to create 3 different doughs:

Pistachio dough

- Add 4 tablespoons of pistachio spread to the mixture and mix well until everything is homogenized, then add 150 g of flour a little at a time, kneading until the dough is smooth and strung;

Chocolate dough

- Add 20 g of cocoa powder, 100 g of flour to the mixture and knead for a few minutes until you get a smooth dough without lumps;

White chocolate dough

- Add 70 g of white chocolate melted in a bain-marie and 130 g of Very strong (bread) flour to the mixture, kneading until stringing;

- Once this is done, form three balls with each of the three types of dough and let them rest for about 3 hours so that they are easier to roll out;
- With each of the three types of dough, form a cylinder with a length of about 50 cm /20" and intertwine them to create a tricolor braid;
- Place the braid in a plum-cake or donut-shaped pan and let it rise until the dough has tripled (it could take about 8 hours);
- Bake in a preheated and ventilated oven at 180°C / 356°F for about 30 minutes or until golden brown;
- Let the braid cool on a wire rack before serving.

5.7 - Il babka

Ingredients

- 120 g of mother yeast
- 300 g of strong (or bread) flour
- 80 g of caster sugar
- 2 eggs
- 110 g of butter at room temperature
- 70 ml of milk
- Vanilla beans
- 1 pinch of salt

Filling:

- 180 g of apricot jam
- 150 g of digestive biscuits
- 50 g of melted butter
- 100 g of chopped dark chocolate

Streusel:

- 30 g of all-purpose (or plain) flour
- 40 g of sugar
- 1/2 teaspoon of cinnamon
- 30 gr of chopped hazelnuts

- 30 g of cold butter

Directions

- Dissolve 120 g of mother yeast together with 80 g of caster sugar, 2 eggs, and 70 ml of milk;
- Operate the planetary mixer and add 110 g of soft butter cut into small pieces, vanilla beans and 1 pinch of salt;
- Once you have a homogeneous mixture, add 300 g of strong (bread) flour a little at a time until it is completely incorporated and bring the dough into stringing;
- Let the dough rise in a bowl covered with cling film until doubled (it will take about 6 hours);
- In the meantime, prepare the streusel by mixing 30 g of flour, 40 g of caster sugar, 1/2 teaspoon of cinnamon, 30 g of chopped hazelnuts, and 30 g of cold butter with your fingertips until you get a sandy and irregular dough, then put it in the fridge;
- Mix 150 g of crumbled digestive biscuits with 50 g of melted butter;
- Divide the leavened dough in two and roll out the two portions with a rolling pin to obtain 2 rectangles of approximately 20 x 30 cm / 8x12";
- Spread on them 180 g of apricot jam, the crumbled biscuits, and 100 g of dark chocolate flakes;
- Roll up the two rectangles starting from the longest side, obtaining two rolls and intertwining them, creating a braid;
- Place it in a plum-cake mold or a donut mold lined with parchment paper and cover with cling film;
- Let the braid rise for about 3 hours until doubled, then decorate the surface with the previously prepared streusel;
- Bake the babka in a preheated static oven at 180°C/350°F with a saucepan of water in the lower part for about 45 minutes until golden brown;
- Cool completely before cutting.

5.8 - The autumn Buccellato

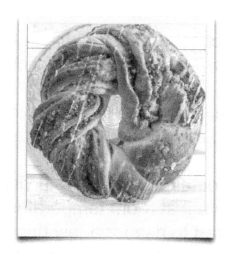

Ingredients

- 160 g of mother yeast
- 250 g of wholemeal flour
- 200 g of very strong (strong bread) flour
- 50 g of chestnut flour
- 220 ml of milk at room temperature
- 120 g of caster sugar
- 1 egg
- 80 g of butter
- 1 pinch of salt
- 100 g of shelled walnuts

Filling:

- 100 g of steamed chestnuts
- 50 g of sultanas

Topping:

- 1 egg yolk
- Milk to taste

Directions

- Dissolve 160 g of mother yeast in 220 ml of milk at room temperature, then add 1 egg, 120 g of caster sugar to the bowl of the mixer and start kneading;
- Add the flour little by little, 50 g of chestnut flour, 1 pinch of salt, and continue to knead at low speed (chestnut flour makes the dough rather delicate);
- When the flour is incorporated, add 80 g of butter at room temperature cut into small pieces, and stir until completely incorporated;
- Place the dough in an airtight container and let it rise overnight until doubled (in winter, leave it at room temperature not too cold, while in summer, let it start to rise for a few hours out of the fridge, and then move it to the fridge for the remaining time);
- When doubled, deflate the dough and add 100 g of shelled walnuts, 100 g of steamed chestnuts in pieces, and 50 g of sultanas previously soaked in warm water, working the dough with your hands;
- Form two loaves by rolling the dough first in one direction and then in the other to give it strength and place them on a baking sheet lined with parchment paper;
- Let it rise for 4-5 hours until doubled in a warm place, then make a deep cut lengthwise;
- Brush the surface with beaten egg yolk and milk;
- Bake at 180°C/350°F in a preheated and ventilated oven for about 25 minutes, until golden brown.
- Let it cool and dry on a rack before serving.

Chapter 6

Cakes

6.1 – Moist bundt cake

Ingredients

Starter:

- 150 g of mother yeast
- 180 g of strong (bread) flour
- 150 ml of water

Main dough:

- Starter
- 180 g of strong (bread) flour
- 160 g of caster sugar
- 3 eggs
- 170 g of peanut oil
- 220 ml of milk
- 120 g di dark cioccolate
- Grated zest of 1 orange
- 1 pinch of salt
- Vanilla bean
- Pearl sugar

Directions

- Dissolve 150 g of mother yeast in 150 ml of water, then add 180 g of previously sifted strong (bread) flour (it will become a liquid dough);
- Cover it with cling film and let it rise at least until doubled (at least 5/6 hours);
- When the starter has doubled, put it in the mixer and start kneading by combining 3 eggs and 160 g of caster sugar;
- When they are incorporated, continue adding 170 ml of peanut oil and 220 ml of milk little at a time stirring constantly to incorporate everything;
- Reduce the speed of the mixer and gradually add 180 g of strong (bread) flour, 1 vanilla bean, the grated zest of 1 orange and, finally, 1 pinch of salt;
- When the dough has reached a smooth and creamy consistency, pour it into a previously greased and floured mold;
- Now cut 120 g of dark chocolate into pieces coarsely, flour them a little and arrange them on the dough (they will fall during cooking);
- Cover the mold with plastic wrap and place it in the fridge overnight;
- In the morning, allow the dough to acclimate and let it continue to rise. It will not grow much in volume but many bubbles will form on the surface;
- After 3/4 hours it will be ready to go in the oven, so sprinkle the surface with pearl sugar;
- Bake in a preheated static oven at 180°C / 356 °F for 40/45 minutes. Use a toothpick to check the cooking, then take it out and let it cool.
- I suggest you serve the moist bundt cake with hazelnut and chocolate cream. You can find the recipe for this delicious cream in chapter 3.

6.2 – Roses cake

Ingredients

- 100 g of mother yeast
- 80 ml of milk at room temperature
- 300 g of very strong (strong bread) flour
- 200 g of strong (bread) flour
- 70 g of caster sugar
- 135 g of butter at room temperature
- 3 eggs

Emulsion:

- 2 tablespoon of honey, 10 g of limoncino (or any liqueur) and the grated zest of 1 orange

Buttercream:

- 100 g of caster sugar, 100 g of butter, the juice of ½ orange

Directions

- In the mixer, add 100 g of mother yeast with 80 ml of milk and 70 g of caster sugar, and mix until the yeast has dissolved;

- Replace the whisk with the leaf, add 300 g of very strong (bread) flour and, once incorporated, add the 3 eggs, one at a time;
- Once the eggs have been incorporated, install the hook and add 200 g of strong (bread) flour, one tablespoon at a time, so that it is incorporated gradually;
- In the meantime, prepare an emulsion consisting of 2 teaspoons of honey, 10 g of liqueur and the grated zest of 1 orange, mixing the ingredients well;
- Add 135 g of butter cut into small pieces, to the emulsion previously prepared and let it knead for another ten minutes until the dough is smooth, homogeneous and strung (you will notice when the dough is rolled on the hook and will be detached from the mixer bowl);
- Put the dough in a hermetically sealed container, which can hold 3 times its volume, and let it rise until it triples (it will take about 10 hours at 26/28 ° C);
- In the meantime, prepare the buttercream with the whisk. Whip together 100 g of caster sugar, 100 g of cold butter cut into small pieces and the juice of ½ orange; the mixture should be soft, white and whipped (it will take 5/10 minutes);
- Once the dough has risen, roll it out on a floured surface, (it should be soft and should be able to roll it out very easily with your hands, without the rolling pin);
- Form a rectangle of about 55 x 45 cm / 22x17", taking care to put plenty of flour in the part in contact with the table, otherwise you will have difficulty in the next step;
- Spread the butter cream evenly on the rectangle of dough;
- Then roll the dough starting from the longest side, in order to obtain a cylinder about 55 cm / 22" long;
- With a very sharp knife cut some washers about 2 / 2.5 cm /0.8" thick (do not cut from top to bottom as you risk flattening the washers. Instead, try to make sharp cuts in the forward / backward direction);
- Place the washers in a round pan with high edges so that they are in contact with each other but not crushed, and let them

rise for about 8-10 hours until they are tripled;

- Bake the rose cake at 180°C / 356°F in a preheated static oven for about 30/35 minutes, until it is golden brown;
- When finished, let it cool and dry on a rack before serving.

I suggest you serve a slice of rose cake with good and soft whipped cream.

6.3 - Brioche chinois with vanilla custard

Ingredients

- 150 g of mother yeast
- 250 g of very strong (strong bread) flour
- 200 g of strong (bread) flour
- 4 eggs
- 100 g of caster sugar
- 110 ml of milk
- 150 g of soft butter
- The grated zest of 1 lemon
- 1 pinch of salt

Filling:

- 300 g of custard
- 100 g of dark chocolate chips

Garnish:

- Pearl sugar or sugar glaze
- Milk

Directions

- First prepare the custard following the recipe in chapter 3, so that it has time to cool down;
- In the meantime, add 150 g of mother yeast, 250 g of very strong (strong bread) flour, 200 g of strong (bread) flour, 100 g of caster sugar, the grated zest of 1 lemon, 110 ml of milk to the mixer and start mixing at low speed;
- The dough will be quite solid at the beginning, so insert 4 eggs one at a time, waiting for the previous one to incorporate well before adding the next;
- When finished with the eggs, add 1 pinch of salt and 150 g of soft butter a little at a time, waiting for it to absorb well before adding more;
- Make the dough string well, turning the planetary mixer for several minutes at low speed (the dough must be smooth, very elastic and fairly soft);
- When it is strung, form a ball, put it in a covered bowl and let it rise until doubled for about 8 hours (if you prefer you can keep it out of the fridge for a couple of hours, then put it in the fridge for the night, in order to start again the next morning);
- When doubled, roll out the dough with a rolling pin, trying to obtain a rectangle about 1 or 2 cm high / 0.8", then spread 300 g of custard over the entire surface, and add 100 g of chocolate chips;
- Roll up the rectangle starting from the long side, obtaining a 50 cm 20" long cylinder;
- Cut it in half and for each half cut 8 washers. Place washers in a round pan with high sides that has been greased or covered with baking paper. Just like the rose cake, place one in the center and the others around it;
- Let it rise until doubled for about 4 hours, then brush the surface with milk and pearl sugar;
- Bake at 170°C / 338 °F in a static oven for about 40 minutes;
- Instead of pearl sugar, you can decorate the cake coming out of the oven with sugar glaze (if you are interested you can consult the recipe in chapter 3).

6.4 - Chestnuts danubio (stuffed Italian rolls)

Ingredients

- 120 g of mother yeast
- 200 g of very strong (bread) flour
- 50 g of chestnut flour
- 50 g of plain (all purpose) flour
- 60 g of caster sugar
- 40 g of butter
- 230 ml of milk
- 1 egg
- 100 g of dark chocolate
- 1 pinch of salt
- 1 vanilla bean

Directions

- Put 120 g of mother yeast and 230 ml of milk in the bowl of the mixer and start mixing at low speed until the yeast is dissolved;
- Add 60 g of caster sugar and continue mixing;
- Make a flour mix consisting of 200 g of very strong (strong bread) flour, 50 g of plain (all-purpose) flour and 50 g of chestnut flour and sift it well;

- Add the flour mix a little at a time in the bowl of the mixer, mixing at low speed;
- Add 1 egg, 1 pinch of salt, the vanilla and continue to knead;
- In the meantime, melt 40 g of butter and once it reaches room temperature, add it to the dough;
- Continue to knead for about 10 minutes with the hook, getting to string the dough;
- Let the dough rest in a bowl for about 20 minutes and reinforce by folding it a few times every 20 minutes, about 3 times in total;
- Place the dough in an airtight container in the refrigerator for about 24 hours;
- Take the dough out of the fridge and divide it into portions of about 50 grams each;
- In the center of each portion of the dough, place a piece of dark chocolate and form a ball using a bit of flour if necessary (approximately 15 balls);
- Place the balls in a round pan with high sides equally spaced by about one centimeter, cover and let them rise for about 12 hours at room temperature;
- Once the balls have tripled their volume, and are touching each other, place the pan in a preheated convection oven at 180°C / 356°F for about 20 minutes, or until your Danubio cake is golden in color;
- When finished, let it cool and dry on a rack before serving.

6.5 – Apple and mascarpone cake

Ingredients

- 120 g of mother yeast
- 400 g of strong (bread) flour
- 150 ml of milk
- 90 g of caster sugar
- 125 g of mascarpone
- 3 apples
- 1 egg
- 1 tablespoon of honey (I used eucalyptus)

Directions

- Dissolve 120 g of mother yeast in 150 ml of milk, 90 g of caster sugar and 1 tablespoon of honey, using a whisk or a planetary mixer;
- Add 1 egg and 125 g of mascarpone and knead until a homogeneous mixture is obtained;
- Peel two apples and cut them into cubes and incorporate them into the mixture, stirring with a spoon;
- Add 400 g of sifted strong (bread) flour 0 a little at a time and continue mixing until you create a nice smooth dough without lumps;

- Let it rise in an airtight container for about 8/10 hours at room temperature;
- Pour the mixture into a plum-cake or donut pan previously lined with parchment paper;
- Peel the third apple, cut it into thin slices and place them on the surface of the dough, covering it completely;
- Let the apple and mascarpone cake rise for about 6 hours until doubled;
- Then sprinkle the surface with pearl sugar and bake in a preheated convection oven at 180°C / 356°F for about 30 minutes, until the cake surface is golden brown (do the stick test to check the doneness);
- When finshed, let it cool and dry on a rack before serving.

6.6 - Cioccolate and chestnut bundt cake

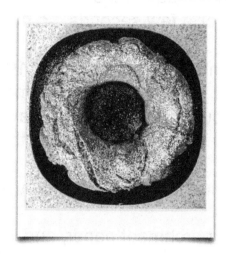

Ingredients

- 120 g of mother yeast
- 130 g of very strong (strong bread) flour
- 30 g of chestnut flour
- 110 ml of milk
- 60 g of caster sugar
- 10 g of bitter cocoa
- 50 g of dark chocolate flakes
- 30 g of butter at room temperature
- 50 g of shelled walnuts

Directions

- Put 120 g of mother yeast, 110 ml of milk, 60 g of caster sugar in the mixer bowl and mix with a whisk until the yeast has dissolved;
- Add 1 pinch of salt, the vanilla and keep stirring;
- In the meantime, mix 30 g of chestnut flour with 130 g of very strong (strong bread) flour and 10 g of cocoa powder;
- Replace the whisk with the leaf and continue to knead adding the flour mix to the main dough a little at a time, finally add 30

g of soft butter cut into small pieces and stir for a few minutes until you create a nice smooth dough without lumps;

- Add 50 g of shelled walnuts and stir for a few seconds, so that they are incorporated into the dough;
- Form a ball and let it rise in an airtight container for about 10-12 hours at room temperature until it increases in volume; (given the presence of chestnut flour, the dough will have difficulty rising but do not despair, it will develop well in the oven);
- At this point, without kneading too much, form a long roll the length of the bundt cake tin;
- Insert the roll into the mold lined with parchment paper, and let it rise for another 8-10 hours at room temperature until doubled;
- Bake the chestnut-chocolate bundt in a ventilated oven at 180°C / 356°F for about 30 minutes until the surface is golden brown (do the stick test to check the doneness);
- When finished, let it cool and dry on a rack before serving.

I suggest you serve a slice with soft Chantilly cream. You can find the recipe for this delicious cream in chapter 3.

6.7 – Trieste Pinza

Ingredients

For the first dough

- 80 g of mother yeast
- 180 g of very strong (strong bread) flour
- 2 egg yolks
- 50 g of melted butter
- 115 ml of water
- 50 g of caster sugar

For the second dough

- 230 g of strong (bread) flour
- 60 g of caster sugar
- 50 ml of peanut oil
- 40 ml of rum
- 40 ml of water
- 10 g of salt
- 1 vial of orange flavoring
- Juice of ½ lemon
- 1 vanilla bean

Directions

I recommend that you start preparing the first dough at around 9pm.

- Dissolve 80 g of mother yeast in 115 ml of water, then add half of the very strong (strong bread) flour (90 g) and let it string;
- Add 50 g of caster sugar, 2 egg yolks, the other half of the very strong (strong bread) flour (90 g) and continue to knead until the dough is strung, then add 50 g of melted butter;
- Once the butter is well incorporated, place the dough in a bowl, put it in a warm place until it has tripled (9-12 hours);
- The following morning, deflate the dough by forming a ball and place it in the fridge to cool for about 1-2 hours;
- Place it in the mixer and start kneading by adding half the strong (bread) flour (115 g), 60 g of caster sugar, 50 ml of peanut oil and 1 vanilla bean;
- Separately mix 40 ml of rum, 40 ml of water, 10 g of salt, 1 vial of orange flavoring and the juice of ½ lemon, then combine everything in the mixer and continue to knead until stringing;
- Transfer the dough onto a floured surface, divide it into two equal parts, form two balls and place them in two small round pans with a low edge. (With this dose there are 2 pliers of 650g cooked weight, but if you prefer you can cook a single one);
- Let rise until doubled (it will take one night - about 8-10 hours);
- Turn on the oven at 200°C / 392°F in static mode and before baking, make a very deep Y cut with a sharp knife on the surface, starting from the center outwards. Brush the entire surface with egg white, even entering the cuts;
- Bake the Trieste Pinza for 20 minutes at 200°C / 392°F, then lower the temperature to 180°C / 356°F and cook for 10 minutes;
- At this point, lower the temperature at 160°C / 320°F and let it cook until the heart reaches a temperature of 94°C / 200°F;
- When finished, place the Pinza to cool on a wire rack.
- I suggest you serve a slice of Trieste Pinza with pistachio cream and white chocolate. You can find the recipe for this

delicious cream in chapter 3.

6.8 - Sweet chestnut and walnut bread

Ingredients

- 120 g of mother yeast
- 110 g of chestnut flour
- 180 g of very strong (strong bread) flour
- 70 g of caster sugar
- 30 g butter
- 150 ml of milk
- 60 g of sultanas
- 60 g of shelled walnuts
- 50 g of dark chocolate chips

Directions

- Start mixing 120 g of mother yeast with 70 g of caster sugar, 30 g of butter cut into small pieces and 150 ml of milk;
- In the meantime, soak the sultanas in a little warm water;
- Gradually add 110 g of chestnut flour and 180 g of very strong (strong bread) flour, previously sieved and mixed together, to the mixture;
- Mix for about 10 minutes trying to develop the gluten mesh as much as possible;
- Once you have a smooth and compact dough, add 50 g of sultanas, 50 g of shelled walnuts, 50 g of dark chocolate chips

and stir for a few seconds;

- Place the mixture in an airtight container at room temperature for 8 hours or overnight;
- Give the loaf the shape you prefer, and let it rise for another 6-8 hours until doubled; (since chestnut flour is present in the dough, it could be more difficult than usual to increase in volume; don't worry, it will increase in volume during cooking);
- Make one or more cuts of about 2 cm /0.8" deep on the surface of the loaf to help development during cooking, and bake in a preheated static oven at 180°C / 356°F for about 30 minutes (if you can't tell if it is baked enough given the dark color of the flour, check that the surface is very hard by tapping it);
- When finished, let it cool and dry on a rack before serving.

Chapter 7

Plum-cakes

7.1 - Walnut and apricot plum-cake

Ingredients

- 100 g of mother yeast
- 110 g of strong (bread) flour
- 110 g of wholemeal flour
- 70 g of caster sugar
- 140 ml of milk
- 1 egg
- 60 g of shelled walnuts
- 70 g of dehydrated apricots
- 1 vanilla bean

Directions

- Put 100 g of mother yeast, 140 ml of milk and 70 g of caster sugar in the mixer bowl and whisk until the yeast has dissolved;
- Add 1 egg, the vanilla and keep stirring;
- In the meantime, sift 110 g of strong (bread) flour with 110 g of wholemeal flour, replace the whisk with the leaf and continue to knead, adding the flour a little at a time to create a nice smooth dough without lumps;
- Add 60 g of shelled walnuts, 70 g of dehydrated apricots and stir for a few seconds, so that they are incorporated into the

dough;

- Let it rise in an airtight container for about 8/10 hours at room temperature;
- Knead the dough a little by rolling it on itself and giving it a cylindrical shape, using a bit of flour, if necessary, then insert it into a plum cake mold, lined with parchment paper;
- Let it rise for another 6 hours at room temperature until doubled;
- Bake the plum cake in a convection oven at 180°C / 356°F for about 30 minutes, until the surface is golden brown (do the toothpick test to check the doneness);
- Once cooked, let it cool and dry on a rack before serving;
- I recommend serving the sliced plum-cake with soft Chantilly cream. You can find the recipe for this delicious cream in chapter 3.

7.2 - Walnut, chocolate and fig plum-cake

Ingredients

- 100 g of mother yeast
- 250 g of strong (bread) flour
- 50 g of wholemeal flour
- 100 g of caster sugar
- 150 ml of milk
- 1 egg
- 1 teaspoon of honey
- 1 vanilla bean
- 1 pinch of salt
- 150 g of fig jam
- 70 g of dark chocolate chips
- 70 g of shelled walnuts

Directions

- Put 100 g of mother yeast, 150 ml of milk, 100 g of caster sugar in the mixer bowl and whisk until the yeast has dissolved;
- Add 1 egg, 1 teaspoon of honey, vanilla and keep stirring;
- In the meantime, sift 50 g of wholemeal flour together with 250 g of strong (bread) flour and 1 pinch of salt;

- Replace the whisk with the leaf and continue kneading, adding the flour mix to the main dough a little at a time, until you create a nice smooth dough without lumps;
- At this point add 70 g of shelled walnuts, 70 g of dark chocolate chips and stir for a few seconds, so that they are incorporated into the dough;
- Let it rise in an airtight container for about 8 hours at room temperature;
- In the meantime, if you are in the right season, I recommend that you prepare the fig jam now, following the recipe for homemade jam that you find in chapter 3;
- Roll out the dough with the rolling pin on a floured surface, obtaining a rectangle of about 15 x 30 cm / 6x12";
- Spread 150 g of fig jam on it, then roll the dough starting from the longest side, obtaining a cylinder the length of your plum cake mold;
- Insert the roll into the mold lined with parchment paper, and let it rise for another 6 hours at room temperature until doubled;
- Bake the plum cake in a convection oven at 180°C / 356°F for about 30 minutes, until the surface is golden brown (if necessary, do a stick test to check the doneness);
- Once cooked, let it cool and dry on a rack before serving.

I suggest you decorate it with white chocolate melted in a bain marie and fresh figs.

7.3 - Yogurt, hazelnut and cocoa plum-cake

Ingredients

- 120 g of mother yeast
- 320 g of very strong (strong bread) flour
- 90 g of caster sugar
- 100 ml of milk
- 30 ml of peanut oil
- 150 ml of white yogurt
- 40 g of unsweetened cocoa powder
- 2 tablespoons of honey
- 70 g of chopped hazelnuts
- 1 pinch of salt

Directions

- Insert 120 g of mother yeast, 100 ml of milk, 90 g of sugar into the bowl of the mixer and mix with a whisk until the yeast has dissolved;
- Add 30 ml of seed oil, 2 tablespoons of honey, 150 g of yogurt and continue to stir;
- In the meantime, mix 320 g of flour with 40 g of unsweetened cocoa and 1 pinch of salt;

- Replace the whisk with the leaf and continue kneading, adding the flour mix to the main dough a little at a time, until you create a nice smooth dough without lumps;
- Add 70 g of chopped hazelnuts and stir for a few seconds, so that they are incorporated into the dough;
- Leave to rest in an airtight container for about 8 hours at room temperature;
- Work the dough a little and roll it on itself to obtain a cylinder the length of the plum cake mold;
- Place the dough into the plum cake mold lined with parchment paper, and let it rise for another 6 hours at room temperature until doubled;
- Bake the yogurt, hazelnut and cocoa plum cake in a convection oven at 180 ° C / 356 ° F for about 30 minutes, until the surface is golden brown (if necessary, test the toothpick to check the doneness);
- Let it cool and dry on a rack before serving.

7.4 - Banana bread

Ingredients

- 90 g of mother yeast
- 150 g of flour plain (all-purpose) flour
- 50 g of wholemeal flour
- 80 g of caster sugar
- 2 eggs
- 80 g of melted butter
- 3 ripe bananas
- 50 g of dark chocolate chips
- 120 g of shelled walnuts
- 1 vanilla bean
- 1 teaspoon of ground cinnamon

Directions

This recipe can be simply prepared by hand, without the use of the planetary mixer.

- In a large bowl, mix the dry ingredients: 150 g of plain (all-purpose) flour and 50 g of wholemeal flour together with 50 g of caster sugar, 1 pinch of salt, 1 teaspoon of cinnamon, 120 g of walnuts and 50 g of dark chocolate chips;

- Separately mix the wet ingredients: 3 mashed ripe bananas, 90 g of mother yeast, 2 eggs, 80 g of melted butter and vanilla;
- Using a rubber spatula, gently mix the dry ingredients together with the wet ingredients, trying not to overwork it as the final result may have a rubbery texture (better that the appearance is a bit lumpy);
- Pour the dough into a plum-cake mold about 10 x 25 cm / 4x10, previously lined with parchment paper;
- Bake the banana bread in a preheated oven at 180 ° C / 356 ° F for 40 minutes, until golden brown. (Insert a toothpick into the center of the banana bread to test for doneness);
- When finished, place it on a rack to cool before serving.

7.5 –Braided chocolate and cream plum-cake

Ingredients

- 120 g of mother yeast
- 280 g of strong (bread) flour
- 100 ml of milk
- 30 g of butter at room temperature
- 50 g caster sugar
- 1 egg
- ½ glass of limoncello (to taste)
- 1 vanilla bean
- 1 pinch of salt
- 70 g of spreadable cream of your preference

Directions

- Put 100 g of mother yeast in 100 ml of milk and 50 g of caster sugar In the mixer bowl and knead until the yeast is dissolved;
- Add half of the flour (140 g), 30 g of butter, 1 egg and continue to knead;
- Add 1 pinch of salt and the rest of the flour (140 g);
- Knead until a soft and homogeneous dough is obtained (5 minutes will be enough);
- Place the dough on a floured surface to rest for 10 minutes;

- Reinforce it by rolling it up on itself a couple of times;
- Put it in an airtight container and let it double at room temperature for about 12 hours;
- Gently deflate it and, pushing it with your fingertips, giving it a rectangular shape of 15 x 50 cm /6x20.
- Spread about 70 g of spreadable cream of your choice on the dough. If you use a very thick cream, such as Nutella to be clear, the dough will tend to stick to the cream, but don't worry, it is not necessary to spread it evenly over the entire surface;
- Once this is done, roll the dough on itself starting from the long side;
- Cut the cylinder in half lengthwise, obtaining two half cylinders and intertwine them on themselves, leaving the most beautiful and decorated part on the outside;
- Place the braid in a baking tray lined with parchment paper, cover it with cling film and let it rise until it has more than doubled (it will take about 6 hours);
- Bake the braid at 180°C / 356°F in a static oven for about 40 minutes, or until golden brown;
- Once cooked, let it cool and dry on a rack before serving.

I suggest you serve a slice of plum-cake intertwined with good, soft whipped cream.

7.6 - Hazelnut and double chocolate plum-cake

Ingredients

- 100 g of mother yeast
- 150 g of very strong (strong bread) flour
- 90 g of wholemeal flour
- 60 g of hazelnut flour
- 1 egg
- 115 ml of warm milk
- 60 g of caster sugar
- 30 g of butter
- 50 g of white chocolate chips
- 30 g of dark chocolate chips
- 1 pinch of salt
- 1 vanilla bean

Directions

- Put 100 g of mother yeast, 115 ml of milk, 60 g of caster sugar in the mixer bowl and whisk until the yeast has dissolved;
- Add 1 egg, 1 pinch of salt, vanilla and keep stirring;

- In the meantime, mix 90 g of wholemeal flour together with 150 g of very strong (strong bread) flour and 60 g of hazelnut flour;
- Replace the whisk with the leaf and continue kneading adding the flour mix to the main dough a little at a time;
- Add 30 g of soft butter cut into small pieces until the dough is smooth and without lumps;
- Add 50 g of white chocolate chips and 30 g of dark chocolate chips and stir for a few seconds so that they are incorporated into the dough;
- Let it rest for 3 hours outside the fridge and then place the mixture in an airtight container for about 8-10 hours in the fridge;
- Roll out the dough with the rolling pin on a floured surface, then roll the dough starting from the longest side, obtaining a cylinder the length of your plum-cake mold;
- Line the plum-cake mold with parchment paper, insert the roll into the mold and let it rise for another 6-8 hours at room temperature until doubled;
- Bake the double chocolate hazelnut plum-cake in a ventilated oven at 180°C / 356°F for about 30 minutes until the surface is golden brown (if necessary, use a toothpick to test for doneness);
- When finished, let it cool and dry on a rack before serving.

Chapter 8

Single portions

8.1 – Braids with ricotta and cherry

Ingredients

- 100 g of mother yeast
- 400 g of strong (bread) flour
- 170 ml of water
- 80 g of caster sugar
- 120 g of ricotta
- Grated zest of 1 lemon
- 1 tablespoon of honey
- 150 g of cherries or strawberries
- 1 pinch of salt

Garnish:

- Caster sugar
- Pearl sugar
- Egg white for brushing

Directions

- Start by mixing 100 g of mother yeast with 170 ml of water, 80 g of caster sugar and 120 g of ricotta;
- When the yeast is dissolved, add the grated zest of 1 lemon, 1 tablespoon of honey, 1 pinch of salt and continue to knead;

- Add 400 g of strong (bread) flour a little at a time until it is all incorporated and knead until the dough is smooth and homogeneous;
- Add 150 g of peeled and chopped fresh cherries and stir for just a few seconds so as not to flake the cherries (you can replace the cherries with strawberries or raisins if you prefer);
- Let the dough rest at room temperature for about 30 minutes;
- Divide the dough into portions of 85 g and form into two long cylinders, then intertwine the two ends to create a small braid;
- Place the braids to rise on a baking tray lined with parchment paper for the whole night (about 8 hours) covered with plastic wrap;
- Brush the surface of the braids with egg white, and sprinkle with granulated sugar and pearl sugar;
- Bake at 170 °C / 338 °F for about 25 minutes until the surface is golden.

8.2 – Fluffy pancakes

Ingredients

- 50 g of mother yeast
- 210 g of plain (all-purpose) flour
- 1 egg
- 240 ml of milk
- 25 g of caster sugar
- 20 ml of rice oil (or peanut oil)
- ½ vanilla bean

Directions

- With a whisk, mix 50 g of mother yeast with 240 ml of milk, 1 egg, ½ vanilla bean and 25 g of sugar until the yeast is dissolved;
- Add 20 ml of rice oil, and then 210 g of plain (all-purpose) flour a little at a time until it is incorporated; (you need to get a creamy, fairly liquid and lump-free mixture);
- Put the mixture in an airtight container and let it rise for a few hours out of the fridge, then place it in the fridge overnight; (In winter, leave the bowl directly at room temperature for 7-8 hours, while in summer it will be ready in 4-5 hours);

- Place a large non-stick pan over medium-high heat and when it is hot, grease it with butter;
- Pour a ladlefull of the prepared pancake mixture in the pan, trying to give the pancake as round a shape as possible (try not to mix the leavened dough, otherwise it will not rise during cooking);
- After a few minutes you will notice bubbles on the top of the pancake, turn it over and finish cooking until golden brown; (adjust the flame, so that the cooking is not too fast and risk burning, but not too slow and risk making it too dry);
- Indulge yourself with the dressing: you can opt for simple Nutella with chopped hazelnuts, or fresh fruit and whipped cream (the choice is yours!);
- If you want to prepare a few more pancakes for the next morning or for the afternoon, you can increase the dose and keep the additional pancakes in the refrigerator, just heat for a few minutes in a pan;

8.3 - Maritozzi with whipped cream

Ingredients

- 150 g of mother yeast
- 200 g of strong (bread) flour
- 100 g of plain (all purpose) flour
- 200 g of very strong (strong bread) flour
- 120 ml of milk
- 120 of caster sugar
- 2 eggs
- 50 ml of peanut oil
- 1 teaspoon of honey
- Juice of one lemon

Directions

- Dissolve 150 g of mother yeast in 120 ml of milk, then add 1 teaspoon of honey and 120 g of caster sugar and continue mixing;
- Incorporate 200 g of flour a little at a time, then 2 lightly beaten eggs;
- Continue to knead, adding 100 g of plain (all purpose) flour a little at a time, 50 ml of peanut oil and lastly the juice of one lemon;

- Knead at least ten minutes, until the dough is smooth, homogeneous and strung;
- Form a ball and let it rest for half an hour, then make a round of folds;
- Place the dough in a covered bowl to rise for 4 to 5 hours, then divide it into 10-12 balls;
- Let them rest, covered, for 20 minutes, then reinforce them again, stretching them and giving them their spherical shape;
- Place them to rise, on a baking tray lined with parchment paper. Allow enough room between them for rising;
- Let the Maritozzi rise for 10-15 hours until the dough has tripled;
- Brush the surface with milk and bake at 180°C / 356°F for about 20 minutes until lightly browned (they must remain fairly soft);
- When the Maritozzi have cooled, cut them lengthwise and fill them with whipped cream. Sprinkle with powdered sugar before serving.

8.4 - Kanelbullar

Ingredients

- 130 g of mother yeast
- 380 g of strong (bread) flour
- 75 g of butter at room temperature
- 250 ml of milk at room temperature
- 40 g of caster sugar
- 2 teaspoons of salt

Filling

- 75 g of butter at room temperature
- 70 g of caster sugar
- 2 teaspoons of ground cinnamon
- 1 beaten egg for brushing
- Pearl sugar

Directions

- Mix 130 g of mother yeast with 75 g of butter, 250 ml of milk, 40 g of caster sugar until the yeast is dissolved;
- Gradually add 380 g of strong (bread) flour and 2 teaspoons of salt and knead until the mixture is smooth and homogeneous;

- Form a ball and let it rise for 4 hours in an airtight container at room temperature;
- When the dough has doubled, roll it out with a rolling pin, obtaining a rectangle of about 50 x 25 cm / 20x10";
- Spread on it 75 g of melted butter, 2 tablespoons of cinnamon, 70 g of caster sugar and roll the rectangle starting from the longest side to obtain a cylinder;
- Cut some rolls to a thickness of about 2.5 cm / 1", place them on a baking tray lined with parchment paper, cover with cling film and let them rise until doubled.
- Once doubled (it will take about 6 hours) brush the surface of the rolls with beaten egg and sprinkle with pearl sugar;
- Bake in a preheated static oven at 200°C / 392°F, until the surface is golden brown.

8.5 - Donuts baked in the oven

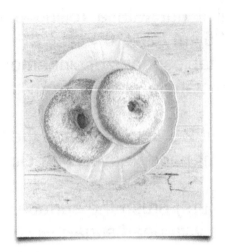

Ingredients

- 180 g of mother yeast
- 150 of strong (bread) flour
- 300 g of very strong (strong bread) flour
- 170 ml of warm milk
- 60 g of caster sugar
- 2 eggs
- Grated zest of ½ lemon
- 1 pinch of salt
- Jam for the filling

Directions

- Start by mixing 180 g of mother yeast with 170 ml of milk, 2 eggs, 60 g of caster sugar and continue until the yeast has dissolved;
- Continue to mix adding the zest of 1 grated lemon, 1 pinch of salt and 150 g of strong (bread) flour a little at a time, until it is all incorporated;
- Finally add 300 g of very strong (strong bread) flour and continue to knead until stringing, then form a ball and place it in an airtight container to rise for about 4 hours;

- Lightly flour the work surface and roll out the dough with a rolling pin to obtain a rectangular sheet of about 0.5 cm / 0.2 inch thick.
- Use a round mold or a large coffee cup to cut dough discs from the rolled sheet of dough;
- On half of the discs, place half a teaspoon of jam in the center, then wet the edges with lukewarm water and cover each filled disc with another disc of dough (Press the edges well with your fingers to seal in the jam);
- Place the donuts on a baking sheet lined with parchment paper, cover with cling film, and leave to rise for about 6-8 hours until doubled;
- Bake in a preheated oven at 180°C / 356°F for about 15 minutes until golden brown;
- Let the donuts cool and sprinkle the surface with powdered sugar

8.6 - Spelt and orange swirl

Ingredients

- 150 g of mother yeast
- 300 g of spelt flour
- 200 g of very strong (strong bread) flour
- 260 ml of milk
- 3 tablespoons of honey
- 2 tablespoons of brown sugar
- 2 eggs
- 80 g of soft butter
- Grated zest of 1 organic orange
- 3 tablespoons of orange jam
- 1 pinch of salt

Garnish:

- 1 tablespoon of water
- ½ squeezed orange
- ½ teaspoon of sugar

Directions

- Mix 150 g of mother yeast together with 300 g of spelt flour and 200 g of very strong (strong bread) flour to obtain a crumbly mixture;

- Combine 260 ml of milk, 1 egg and continue to knead;
- Add 3 tablespoons of honey, 2 tablespoons of brown sugar, the other egg and run the planetary mixer for a few more minutes;
- When the mixture is homogeneous, add 1 pinch of salt, the zest of an orange, 80 g of soft butter cut into small pieces and string the dough;
- At this point, place it in the fridge for at least two hours (or even better overnight) so that it can relax and make processing easier;
- Take the dough out of the fridge and bring it to room temperature. Roll it out with a rolling pin to obtain a rectangle of about 50 x 30 cm / 20x12", less than 1 cm /0.4" thick;
- Spread 3 tablespoons of orange marmalade evenly on the surface, then roll up the rectangle starting from the long side, obtaining a roll about 50 cm / 20" long;
- Cut some 1.5 cm /0.6" high swivels and put them to rise on a baking tray lined with parchment paper at about 25°C / 77°F for 6-8 hours until doubled;
- Bake the spelt and orange rolls in a preheated convection oven at 180°C / 356°F for about 15 minutes, until golden;
- As soon as they come out of the oven, brush the surface with orange syrup, obtained by mixing 1 tablespoon of water, ½ squeezed orange and ½ teaspoon of sugar.

8.7 – Chocolate rolls

Ingredients

- 150 g of mother yeast
- 70 g of potato flakes
- 200 g of plain (all-purpose) flour
- 300 g of very strong (strong bread) flour
- 3 eggs
- 70 g of soft butter
- 250 ml of milk
- 50 g of caster sugar
- 1 teaspoon of salt
- Nutella to taste

Directions

- Start by mixing 70 g of potato flakes with half of the warmed milk (125 ml);
- In another bowl dissolve 150 g of yeast together with the remaining milk (125 ml), then add 3 eggs, 50 g of caster sugar, 70 g of soft butter and start mixing;
- When the yeast is dissolved, add the softened potato flakes, and continuing to knead, gradually add 200 g of plain (all-

purpose) flour, 300 g of very strong (strong bread) flour and 1 teaspoon of salt;

- Continue to knead with the hook until the mixture comes off the walls, then place it in an airtight container to rise at 25°C / 77°F for 5 hours until it has tripled;
- Roll out the leavened dough on a floured work surface without handling it too much (you will need to get a fairly large rectangle with a thickness of about 1-2 cm /0.6" from which to obtain 9 or 12 rectangles);
- In each rectangle place a chocolate strip on the long part and start rolling the rectangle, reaching the middle. At this point, make 5 or 6 "comb" cuts on the remaining flap of dough and finish with rolling;
- Place the flutes in a pan with space between them and let them rise for 2-3 hours at room temperature covered with a cloth;
- When doubled, brush the surface with 1 egg yolk beaten with a drop of milk and bake in a convection oven preheated to 180°C / 356°F for 15-20 minutes until golden brown.

8.8 - Peach and custard Danish brioche

Ingredients

- 150 g of mother yeast
- 400 g of strong (bread) flour
- 100 g of very strong (strong bread) flour
- 150 ml of water
- 2 eggs
- 30 g of butter at room temperature
- 70 g of caster sugar
- 1 teaspoon of honey
- The juice of 1 orange
- Syrup packed peaches to taste
- 2 cup of custard (see chapter 3)
- 1 envelope unflavored gelatin (about 1 tablespoon)

Directions

- First prepare the custard following the recipe you find in chapter 3 so that it has time to cool down;
- Dissolve 150 g of yeast with 1/3 of the water (50 ml), 1 teaspoon of honey and let it rest for half an hour;
- Then combine in sequence 70 g of sugar, 2 eggs, the juice of 1 orange, continuing to knead;

- Add the remaining 100 ml of water, then 400 g of plain flour and 100 g of very strong flour a little at a time;
- Once the dough has become smooth and homogeneous, add 30 g of soft butter cut into small pieces and knead for a few more minutes until stringing;
- Let it rise at room temperature for half an hour and then place the dough in an airtight container in the fridge for about 10 hours;
- Remove it from the fridge and after half an hour roll out the dough on a floured surface to form a fairly large rectangle with a thickness of 3mm;
- From this make squares of 10x10cm / 4x4" by cutting the pastry with a wheel and pour a generous teaspoon of custard in the center of each;
- Score the four edges by cutting them in half until you almost reach the center of the square, then fold the tips towards the center thus forming pinwheels;
- Place them on a baking tray lined with parchment paper and place a few slices of peach in syrup in the center of each swivel;
- Bake in a convection oven at 180°C / 355°F for 10-15 minutes until golden brown;
- Once taken out of the oven, brush them with ready-made gelatin and let them cool on a rack before serving.

8.9 – Nutella roll

Ingredients

- 110 g of mother yeast
- 350 g of strong (bread) flour
- 55 g of caster sugar
- 175 ml of milk
- 55 g of melted butter
- 1 pinch of salt
- Nutella to taste

Directions

- Start by mixing 110 g of mother yeast with 175 ml of milk, 55 g of sugar and continue until the yeast has dissolved;
- Continue to mix adding 350 g of flour a little at a time and a pinch of salt until all is incorporated;
- Finally add 55 g of melted butter cut into small pieces and continue to knead until stringing;
- Form a ball and place it in an airtight container to rise at about 25°C / 75°F for about 4 hours;
- Once doubled, take the dough, divide it into 10-12 pieces and roll them out to form rectangles;
- Stuff them with Nutella, then roll them up well and twist the cylinder on itself to form an egg;

- Place the snails on the baking tray lined with parchment paper spaced apart, sprinkle the surface with sugar and let it rise for about 8 hours until doubled;
- Bake the Nutella rolls in a convection oven at 180°C / 355°F for about 10-15 minutes until golden brown.

8.10 – Chocolate chips bun

•

Ingredients

- 150 g of mother yeast
- 290 g of very strong (strong bread) flour
- 225 g of plain (all purpose) flour
- 100 g of water
- 110 g of milk at room temperature
- 90 g of caster sugar
- 50 g of soft butter
- 130 g of dark chocolate chips
- 1 teaspoon of wildflower honey
- 1 egg
- 1 vanilla bean
- 1 pinch of salt

To brush:

- 1 yolk
- 1 tablespoon of milk

Directions

- Place 150 g of mother yeast, 110 ml of milk, 100 ml of water, and 1 teaspoon of honey into the bowl of the mixer and turn it until the yeast is dissolved;
- Add 90 g of sugar, 1 egg, 1 pinch of salt, vanilla and continue mixing;
- Combine 290 g of very strong flour a little at a time in the bowl of the mixer, mixing at low speed;
- Add 50 g of butter cut into small pieces, 225 g of plain flour and continue to knead for about 10 minutes until the dough is strung;
- Finally, add 130 g of dark chocolate chips and turn at low speed so that they are incorporated into the dough;
- Place the dough in an airtight bowl and leave it at room temperature for 1 hour, then in the refrigerator for 12 hours;
- Towards evening, divide the dough into balls of 50 g each and let them rest for two hours covered with cling film;
- Strengthen the balls, giving them back their spherical shape, place them on the pan with enough space between them, cover with cling film and let them rise overnight;
- Mix 1 egg yolk and 1 tablespoon of milk and gently brush the surface of each roll;
- Bake in a preheated ventilated oven at 160°C / 320°F for about 15 minutes until golden brown.

8.11 - Cinnamon roll

Ingredients

- 150 g of mother yeast
- 160 g of very strong (strong flour) flour
- 125 g of strong (bread) flour
- 170 ml of milk
- 35 g of caster sugar
- 40 g of butter at room temperature
- 1 teaspoon of honey
- 125 ml of yogurt
- 1 vanilla bean
- 1 teaspoon of salt
  For the filling:
- 40 g of butter at room temperature
- 1 generous teaspoon of ground cinnamon
- 75 g of caster sugar

Directions

- Put 150 g of mother yeast, 170 ml of milk, 1 teaspoon of honey, 35 g of sugar and 25 ml of yogurt in the bowl of the mixer and start kneading;

- After a few minutes add 160 g of very strong flour, 125 g of strong flour, 1 vanilla bean and 1 teaspoon of salt;
- When the dough is homogeneous, add 40 g of butter cut into small pieces and let it turn until it is completely absorbed;
- Place the dough in an airtight container and let it rise overnight at room temperature (about 8 hours);
- In the morning, prepare the buttercream by whipping 40 g of butter at room temperature, 1 generous teaspoon of cinnamon and 75 g of granulated sugar with an electric whisk;
- On a floured work surface, roll out the dough with a rolling pin to obtain a rectangle shape;
- Spread the buttercream and cinnamon on it and then roll the rectangle over it, starting from the longest side.
- Cut 3 cm thick / 1" washers trying not to ovalize them during cutting (they should be about 15);
- Place them on a baking tray, well-spaced apart, cover them with cling film and let them rise for about another 6 hours, until they are tripled;
- Bake your cinnamon rolls in a preheated convection oven at 170°C / 340°F for about 30 minutes or until golden brown.

8.12 - Pistachio brioche

Ingredients

- 150 g of mother yeast
- 180 g of very strong (strong bread) flour
- 60 g of mixed cereal or wholemeal flour
- 70 g of unsalted roasted pistachios
- 50 g of butter at room temperature
- 80 g of caster sugar
- 125 ml of fresh whole milk
- 1 teaspoon of honey
- 1 egg
- 1 pinch of salt
- 1 vanilla bean

Pistachio glaze:

- 50 g of pistachio spread cream
- 100 g of white chocolate

Directions

(I recommend starting the preparation in the evening)

- In a mixer dissolve 150 g of mother yeast in 125 ml of milk, 50 g of butter at room temperature and 80 g of sugar;

- After a few minutes, add 1 teaspoon of honey, 1 egg, 1 pinch of salt and the vanilla, continuing to knead;
- Gradually add 180 g of flour and 60 g of flour until they are completely incorporated;
- Finally add 70 g of unsalted roasted pistachios and stir for a few seconds;
- Leave the dough to rise in an airtight container for about 8 hours until doubled;
- Divide the dough into 50 g loaves, then form the brioches, rolling the loaves on themselves first in one direction and then in the other;
- Place them on one or more trays lined with parchment paper, cover them with cling film and place them in the fridge for about 18 hours;
- Take the pans out of the fridge and let the leavening finish for another 6 hours at room temperature until they have tripled;
- Bake in a preheated, ventilated oven at 180°C / 355°F for about 15 minutes until golden brown;
- Cool the brioches on a wire rack, and in the meantime, put 20 ml of fresh liquid cream in a saucepan over low heat until lightly boiling;
- Turn off the heat and continue to mix while adding 100 g of white chocolate and then 50 g of pistachio spread, until you get a smooth and shiny cream. With a spoon, pour the icing on the surface of the brioches, and finish with a light rain of chopped pistachios.
- Allow to cool until the icing is dry.

8.13- Wee carrot cake

Ingredients

- 80 g of mother yeast
- 250 g of very strong (strong bread) flour
- 90 g of almond flour
- 70 g of caster sugar
- 70 ml of warm water
- 150 g of grated carrots (about 2)
- 1 egg
- 1 tablespoon of wildflower honey
- 1 vanilla bean
- 1 pinch of salt
- Pearl sugar to taste

Directions

- Dissolve 80 g of mother yeast in 70 ml of warm water, 1 tablespoon of honey and 70 g of sugar;
- Add 1 egg, half the very strong flour (125 g) and continue to knead, then add 1 vanilla bean, 1 pinch of salt and continue to turn the mixer;
- Add the other half of the flour (125 g) a little at a time and let it turn until the dough is strung;

- Add 150 g of grated carrots and mix gently until they are incorporated into the dough;
- Make the dough into a ball and place it in an airtight container to rise for 2 hours and then transfer it to the fridge for another 8 hours;
- Take the dough out of the fridge, divide it into 60 g portions and form into balls. Place them on one or more trays with plenty of space between them and cover with cling film;
- Let it rise until doubled in volume (about 6 hours) after which decorate the surface with sugar grains;
- Bake the wee carrot cakes in a convection oven at 180°C / 350°F for 15 minutes until golden brown.

8.14- Coconut roll

Ingredients

- 100 g of mother yeast
- 160 g of plain (all purpose) flour
- 50 g of grated coconut
- 65 g of sugar
- 65 ml of water
- 25 g of butter at room temperature
- 100 g of mascarpone
- 1 egg
- 1 vanilla bean
- 1 pinch of salt
- 30 g of blackberries for decoration

Directions

- Start by preparing the blackberry (or raspberry) jam following the recipe for homemade jam you find in chapter 3;
- In the meantime, dissolve 100 g of mother yeast in 65 ml of water, 100 g of mascarpone, 1 egg, 65 g of sugar and mix until the yeast is dissolved;

- Add 25 g of soft butter cut into small pieces, 1 vanilla bean, 1 pinch of salt and continue to mix;
- Add 160 g of plain flour and 50 g of grated coconut, a little at a time while continuing to knead;
- Once the mixture is homogeneous (it will be rather soft) form a ball and let it rest for about 1 hour;
- Roll out the dough with a rolling pin to create a rectangle of about 50 x 30 cm 20/12" and spread the room temperature blackberry jam on top of the dough;
- Roll up the rectangle starting from the longest part, then cut the loaf into slices with a thickness of about 2 cm /0.8", trying not to flatten them during cutting;
- Place the swivels on one or more baking sheets covered with parchment paper and let them rise for about 8 hours or until doubled;
- Bake the blackberry and coconut rolls in a preheated and ventilated oven at 160°C / 320°F for about 20 minutes until golden brown;
- When cooled, decorate the rolls with a few blackberries and serve with whipped cream.

8.15- Babà: Neapolitan brioche

Ingredients

- 120 g of mother yeast
- 200 g of very strong (strong bead) flour
- 120 g of strong (bread) flour
- 4 medium whole eggs
- 2 egg yolks
- 25 g of sugar
- 80 g of butter
- 1 pinch of salt
- Ingredients for the syrup:
- 800 ml of water
- 400 g of caster sugar
- 300 g of rum
- 4 cm /1.5" diameter and 6 cm /2.5" high molds

Directions

- Start by beating 4 eggs, 2 egg yolks and 25 g of sugar with 120 g of mother yeast;
- Add 200 g of very strong flour and 1 pinch of salt and continue to knead;
- Add 120 g of strong flour and stir for a few minutes;

- Now add 80 g of softened butter a little at a time and knead for about 5 minutes until the dough is smooth and homogeneous;
- Form a ball, place it in an airtight container and let it rise for about 3 hours;
- Turn the dough over on a greased pastry board and with buttered hands round the dough several times in your hands, forming a ball again. Let it rest for another 20 minutes (For sizing them, I suggest you use molds of **4 cm /1.5" diameter and 6 cm /2.5" high**);
- Squeeze the dough between your forefinger and thumb and cut into 50g balls, round them and arrange them with the cut part in contact with the mold. (To do this, place the ball on the palm of your hand with the cut side facing the other and roll it into the mold);
- Place the molds on a baking tray, cover them with cling film and let them rise until they reach the edge (about 3/4 hours);
- Once leavened, bake the babà in a preheated static oven at 180°C /355°F for about 25 minutes (After the first 10/15 minutes, place aluminium foil over the babas they do not darken too much);

In the meantime, prepare the syrup:

- Boil 800 ml of water with 400 g of sugar;
- When the sugar is dissolved, turn off the heat, add 300 ml of rum and let it cool;
- Remove the babas from the oven, let them cool for half an hour in the molds and then unmold them while still warm;
- Dip them into the rum bath (which must also be lukewarm) and leave them until they are well soaked, then squeeze them lightly;
- Let them cool completely upside down on a plate or baking tray, then put them in the fridge for a couple of hours before serving;

They can be enjoyed on their own or garnished with cream and fruit or custard and fruit depending on your taste.
Soaked babas can be kept in the fridge for up to three days. If you want to keep the babas for other occasions, do not soak them, put them in a plastic food bag, in this way they will keep for a week.

8.16- Swedish baked Krapfen

Ingredients

"Biga" dough

- 60 g of mother yeast
- 250 g of strong (bread) flour
- 100 ml of milk

Main dough:

- Biga dough
- 150 g of very strong (or strong bread) flour
- 40 g of caster sugar
- 1 egg yolk
- 50 g of butter at room temperature
- 1 teaspoon of vanilla powdered sugar
- 70 ml of milk
- 1 pinch of salt.

Filling

- Classic or chocolate custard (find the recipe in chapter 3)

Directions

- First of all, I suggest you prepare the classic or chocolate custard following the recipe you find in chapter 3. You will need it to fill your Swedish donuts;
- Start by preparing the biga: dissolve 60 g of yeast in 100 ml of milk, then add 250 g of very strong flour a little at a time without mixing too much (you need to get a raw and not compact mixture but in small pieces);
- Put the biga in a bowl covered with cling film and let it ferment at room temperature at about 20°C / 68°F until the next day, for about 18 hours;
- Put the biga dough into the mixer and let the hook turn for a few seconds, then add 1 egg yolk, followed by 40 g of sugar and 1 pinch of salt;
- Add 70 ml of warm milk and 150 g of strong flour and knead until the dough has taken on body;
- Finally add 50 g of soft butter cut into small pieces and turn until it is completely incorporated (if the dough seems too dry, add 1 tablespoon of milk);
- Form a ball, place it in an airtight container and let it rest for about 30 min;
- Divide the dough into pieces of about 60-65 g each, round them slightly, trying not to mix the dough, and cover them with plastic wrap as you prepare them;
- As soon as the portioning is done, start filling them:
- Slightly flatten the balls and place a teaspoon of classic or chocolate custard in the center, then close the flaps tightly and round into a ball. Arrange the donuts on a baking sheet lined with separate pieces of parchment paper and let them rise for 3 or 4 hours until doubled in volume;
- When the leavening is complete, bake the donuts in the oven in static mode at 220°C / 420°F for 6-8 min until golden brown;
- As soon as they are baked, brush them with melted butter and sprinkle with powdered or granulated sugar.

You can also fill the donuts after cooking!

Chapter 9

Biscuits

9.1- Cardamom biscuits

Ingredients

- 100 g of mother yeast
- 150 g of wholemeal flour

  - 150 g of strong (bread) flour
  - 130 ml of almond milk

- 60 g of cane sugar
- 120 g of butter at room temperature
- 1 pinch of salt
- 1 teaspoon of cardamom powder
- 1 beaten egg for brushing

Directions

- In the bowl of the planetary mixer, add 100 g of mother yeast, 60 g of brown sugar and start mixing;
- When the yeast is dissolved, add 130 ml of almond milk gradually, continuing to knead;
- Now add the mix of the two flours a little at a time, along with 1 teaspoon of cardamom powder and 1 pinch of salt. Turn until you get a homogeneous mixture;

- At this point, gradually incorporate 120 g of butter at room temperature until a homogeneous mass is obtained;
- Form a ball and let it rest for 30 minutes in the planetary mixer;
- Make a round of reinforcement folds, form a ball again and leave to rise for about 3 hours at room temperature in an airtight bowl;
- Roll out the dough on a surface without using flour (since it is a fatty dough it will not stick to the surface) and cut strips about 10 cm /4" long and form small loaves;
- Close the two ends forming a small bowl, dip them in granulated sugar, place them on a baking tray covered with parchment paper and cover them with cling film;
- Once doubled (after about 3-4 hours) brush the surface with 1 beaten egg and bake them in a preheated static oven at 180°C / 355°F for about 15-20 minutes until golden brown.

9.2- Apple biscuits

Ingredients

- 130 g of mother yeast
- 200 g of wholemeal flour
- 50 g of strong (bread) flour
- 50 g of very strong (strong bread) flour
- 150 g of white yogurt
- 1 egg
- 65 g of caster sugar
- Grated zest of 1 lemon
- 1 pinch of salt
  Filling
- 2 apples
- 2 tablespoons of orange marmalade
- 30 g of sugar
- 1 pinch of cinnamon

Directions

- Start by creating a mix of flours consisting of 200 g of wholemeal flour, 50 g of very strong flour and 50 g of strong flour, sieving and mixing them together;

- In the bowl of the mixer, lightly beat 1 egg with 65 g of sugar and add 150 g of white yogurt and 130 g of mother yeast;
- Add the flour mix a little at a time, continuing to mix until everything is incorporated, then add the grated zest of 1 lemon;
- Continue to knead for a few minutes until you get a homogeneous strung dough without lumps;
- Form a ball and put it in the fridge for about half an hour covered with cling film;
- In the meantime, cut 2 apples into pieces and stew them for ten minutes with 2 tablespoons of orange marmalade, 30 g of sugar and a pinch of cinnamon, over low heat covered with a lid;
- Take the mass from the refrigerator, divide it into two equal parts and roll out both to obtain two sheets about 0.5 cm /0.2" thick; Place the first sheet on a floured surface, then with a teaspoon, place mounds of (cooled) jam equally spaced on it, then cover it with the second sheet (calculate the distance between the mounds of jam according to the size of the cookie cutter used);
- With a mold, cut the dough forming the biscuits, making sure that the jam is exactly in the center of them;
- Place biscuits on a baking tray covered with parchment paper and leave to rise for about 3-4 hours until doubled. Bake in a preheated static oven at 180°C / 355°F for about 10-15 minutes until golden brown.

9.3- Multigrain rusk

Ingredients

- 180 g of mother yeast
- 200 g very strong (strong bread) flour
- 100 g of wholemeal flour
- 100 g of spelt flour
- 100 g of mixed grain flour
- 60 g of wildflower honey
- 250 ml of milk
- 6 g of salt
- 50 ml of Evo oil
- 50 g of puffed spelt flakes

Directions

- Sift all flours and mix in the planetary mixer;
- Add 180 g of mother yeast, 250 ml of milk, 60 g of wildflower honey and start kneading;
- When the flour is incorporated, add 6 g of salt and 50 ml of oil of oil a little at a time until you get a smooth and strung dough;
- Leave the dough in the bowl for about an hour, then make reinforcing folds, give it the ball shape again and put it to rise in an airtight container at about 24°C /76°F for 2 hours;

- Roll out the dough with a rolling pin to form a rectangle, distribute a layer of spelled flakes on the surface and roll the rectangle starting from the short side (the length of the roll will be equal to the length of the plum-cake mold);
- Slightly moisten the outer surface of the roll with water and apply a layer of spelled flakes on it. Place it in a plum cake mold covered with parchment paper;
- Cover the mold with cling film and let it rise until doubled in volume in a warm and sheltered place (it will take about 8 hours);
- Once risen, brush the surface with milk, and bake in a static oven preheated to 180°C / 355°F for about 30-35 minutes (if it is too dark on the surface, cover it with a sheet of aluminium foil);
- Take it out of the oven and let it cool for about 15 minutes, then gently remove it from the mold and place it on a rack to allow it to dry thoroughly;
- You will be tempted to eat it as it is, but I recommend that you continue to prepare splendid multigrain rusks;
- Wrap the loaf in a tea towel and wait at least 12 hours before cutting it into slices so that it loses any residual moisture;
- Cut the loaf into slices of the same thickness, place them on the grill or dripping pan of the oven and toast them in a static oven preheated at 140°C / 280°F for about 40-45 minutes, turning them halfway through roasting (observe the progress of the toasting, making sure they do not get too dark);
- Turn off the oven but do not take them out immediately: leave them inside a little longer to dry, with the oven door half open, then take them out of the oven and let them cool completely in the air.
- When they are cold, place the rusks in a tightly closed food bag or tin cans. They will keep for a long time, even 3-4 weeks.

9.4- Multigrain Italian rusk

Ingredients

- 120 g of mother yeast
- 250 g of very strong (strong bread) flour
- 150 g of multi grain flour
- 50 g of caster sugar
- 80 ml of milk
- 50 g of butter at room temperature
- 1 egg white
- 1 vanilla bean

Directions

- Start preparing the leaven by mixing 120 g of mother yeast, 80 ml of milk, and 150 g of flour with the multi grain flour and let it rise until doubled (it will take about 2-3 hours);
- Now add 250 g of very strong flour, 50 g of butter cut into small pieces, 50 g of sugar, 1 egg white and 1 vanilla bean to the yeast and knead everything until you get a firm and smooth dough (you should get a firm and plastic dough - if necessary, adjust the consistency by adding a little flour or a drop of milk);
- Form a ball and let it rest covered with a cloth for half an hour;

- Divide it into 2 parts and roll them up on themselves on the work surface until you get two strands with a diameter of 4-5 cm /1.8", then cover them and let them rise for 3 hours until doubled;
- Bake the loaves in a preheated static oven at 180°C / 355°F for 30 minutes until golden brown;
- When finished, let them cool covered with a cloth for about 24 hours so that they dry well;
- Slice the loaves on the bias in order to obtain thin slices that you will bake again in the oven at 140°C / 280°F until they are completely dry and beautifully colored;
- Once the biscuits have been cooked, leave them in the oven with the door ajar until it is cold.

You can enjoy the biscuits by spreading jam or hazelnut cream on the top.

When they are cold, place the biscuits in a tightly closed food bag or tin can. They will keep for a long time, even 3-4 weeks.

9.5- Cream filled cookies

Ingredients

- 120 g of mother yeast
- 100 g of wholemeal flour
- 150 g of very strong (strong bread) flour
- 70 g of buckwheat flour
- 120 g of butter at room temperature
- 120 g of cane sugar
- 2 tablespoons of honey
- 1 teaspoon of cinnamon
- 2 small eggs

Ingredients for the filling:

- Jam or spreadable cream to taste
- 4 tablespoons of toasted almonds

Directions

- In the bowl of the planetary mixer, add 120 g of mother yeast, 120 g of brown sugar, 120 g of soft butter cut into small pieces and start kneading;
- Make a flour mix consisting of 100 g of wholemeal flour, 150 g of very strong flour, 70 g of buckwheat flour and gradually add it to the dough;

- Finally add 2 tablespoons of honey, 1 teaspoon of cinnamon and 2 small eggs, continuing to knead until the dough is smooth and homogeneous (you should get a firm and plastic dough - if necessary, adjust the consistency by adding a little flour or a drop of milk);
- Place the dough in the fridge for 45 minutes to rest;
- Roll it out with a rolling pin, obtaining a sheet of 0.5 cm / 0.2" thick;
- Cut out some circles with the help of molds or a glass, then fill half of them with a portion of Nutella in the center, being careful not to dirty the outside which otherwise will not seal;
- Top with the other half of the circles, make them adhere well on the edges by pressing with your fingers;
- Place the cookies on a baking tray lined with parchment paper, decorate the surface of the cookies with chopped almonds and cover everything with cling film;
- Let it rise until doubled in volume for about two hours;
- Bake the cookies in a preheated static oven at 180°C / 335°F for 20/25 minutes until golden brown. They will remain nice and soft thanks to the Nutella filling.

9.6- Figs and spelt biscuits

Ingredients

- 120 g of mother yeast
- 200 g of wholemeal spelled flour
- 100 g of very strong (strong bread) flour
- 130 g of butter
- 110 g of cane sugar
- 1 egg
- About 30ml of milk - just enough to mix
- Fig jam to taste

Directions

- In the bowl of the planetary mixer, add 120 g of mother yeast, 110 g of brown sugar, 130 g of soft butter cut into small pieces and start kneading;
- Make a flour mix consisting of 200 g of wholemeal spelled, 100 g of very strong flour, and gradually add it to the dough;
- Finally add 1 egg and about 30 ml of milk, continue to knead until the dough is smooth and homogeneous (you should get a firm and plastic dough - if necessary, adjust the consistency by adding a little flour or a drop of milk);
- Place the dough in the fridge for 1 hour to rest;

- Roll it out with a rolling pin, obtaining a sheet of 0.5 cm / 0.2" thick;
- Spread the fig jam over the entire surface, then fold the sheet in half and place it on a tray covered with cling film to rise for 3 hours;
- At this point, bake the filled pastry at 160°C / 320°F for 30-35 minutes;
- After 20 minutes of baking, take it out, cut very gently into large 2x5 cm /0.8x2" strips, taking care not to crumble the dough;
- Put the fig biscuits back in the oven for another 15-20 minutes until they are golden on the surface.

Chapter 10

The fried doughs

10.1 – Italian donuts

Ingredients

- 60 g of mother yeast
- 180 of strong (bread) flour
- 30 g of caster sugar
- 110 ml of water
- 1 pinch of salt
- Peanut oil for frying
- Powdered sugar for topping

Directions

- Dissolve 60 g of yeast in 110 ml of water and 30 g of sugar;
- Add 180 g of flour a little at a time and 1 pinch of salt and continue to knead until the dough is smooth and homogeneous;
- Form a ball, let it rest at room temperature for 1 hour, then place it in an airtight container in the refrigerator for about 8 hours (or overnight);
- Take the dough out of the fridge, let it acclimate for 2 hours and then start forming donuts:
- Cut 30 g pieces of dough and form loaves, then join the two edges, creating a ring;

- Place the donuts on a baking sheet on top of pieces of parchment paper separated one from the other so that they are easier to handle without damaging the leavening, then cover the pan with cling film and let it rise for 4-5 hours;
- Heat an abundant amount of peanut oil to 180°C / 355°F and fry the donuts until golden Brown. (Be careful not to overcook, otherwise they will become too dry. Cook only a few at a time to keep the temperature of the oil controlled. It must be constant and must not drop too much in temperature);
- Once cooked, drain and dip them in granulated sugar.

10.2 – Fried dough balls

Ingredients

- 110 g of mother yeast
- 260 g of strong (bread) flour
- 200 ml of warm water
- 30 ml of grappa (liqueur) to taste
- 40 g of caster sugar
- 80 g of sultanas
- The grated zest of 1 lemon
- Peanut oil for frying
- 15 g of caster sugar for topping

Directions

- First, place 80 g of sultanas in a glass of warm soaking water;
- Dissolve 110 g of mother yeast in 200 ml of water and 40 g of sugar;
- Add 260 g of flour a little at a time, the grated zest of 1 lemon and continue to knead for a few minutes;
- Add the liqueur to the dough and continue to knead until the mixture is smooth and homogeneous;
- Put the mixture in an airtight container to rise at room temperature for 4-5 hours;

- Incorporate 80 g of dried sultanas by gently kneading the dough;
- Let the dough rest for about 1 hour at room temperature (the dough will be rather soft and sticky);
- Heat plenty of peanut oil to 180°C / 355°F, then with the help of two greased teaspoons, form balls that you will slide into the boiling oil. (Take care to cook a few at a time and to keep the temperature of the oil under control. The oil temperature must be constant and not drop too much);
- Fry the dough until well puffed and golden. Once cooked, dry on absorbent paper and roll in sugar before serving them hot.

The classic recipe calls for the addition of 50 g of pine nuts and 50 g of candied citron, to be added to the dough after rising. But as you know, each preparation must be adapted to the tastes of those who have to eat it.

10.3 – Krapfen super star

Ingredients

- 110 g of mother yeast
- 260 g of very strong (strong bread) flour
- 100 g of plain (all purpose) flour
- 230 ml of warm milk
- 50 g of caster sugar
- 1 egg
- 40 g of butter at room temperature
- 1 pinch of salt
- Peanut oil for frying

Directions

- Dissolve 110 g of mother yeast in 230 ml of milk;
- Add 50 g of sugar, 1 egg and 40 g of butter while continuing to knead;
- Make a flour mix consisting of 260 g of very strong flour and 100 g of plain flour, sift it and add it to the dough a little at a time;
- Once all the flour has been incorporated, add 1 pinch of salt and continue kneading until the dough is smooth and homogeneous;

- Form a ball, place it in an airtight bowl and after leaving it at room temperature for 1 hour, place it in the fridge for 12 hours;
- The next day remove the bowl from the fridge, let it acclimate for a few hours;
- Roll out the dough to a height of 1.5 /0.6" and with a pastry cutter or a glass cut circles of dough;
- Place them on a cutting board, resting on some pieces of parchment paper so that they are separated from each other and cover them with cling film;
- Let them rise for about 3-4 hours at 25°C / 77°C until doubled in volume;
- Place the donuts in the fridge for 15 minutes to cool them a little, trying not to damage the leavening;
- In the meantime, put a saucepan with plenty of peanut oil on the heat until it reaches 170°C / 340°F, then immerse the donuts taken directly from the fridge, gently detaching them from the pieces of parchment paper. (Take care to cook a few at a time and keep the temperature of the oil constant);
- Drain the donuts, dip them in sugar and serve them.

10.4 – Fried cannolo

Ingredients

- 150 of mother yeast
- 300 g of very strong (strong bread) flour
- 80 g of strong (bread) flour
- 50 g of butter at room temperature
- 1 egg
- 180 of cold milk
- 55 g of caster sugar
- 10 g of condensed milk
- 5 g of salt
- 1 vanilla bean
- 12 aluminum cylinders for cannoli
- Peanut oil for frying
  Filling:
- 500 g of sheep's milk ricotta (or cow's milk)
- 180 of sugar
- 50 g of chocolate chips

Directions

- Sift 300 g of very strong flour and 80 g of strong flour and place them in a planetary mixer;

- Add 50 g of butter cut into small pieces, the vanilla and continue mixing;
- Add 150 g of mother yeast, 55 g of sugar, 180 ml of milk and continue to knead;
- Finally, add 10 g of condensed milk, 5 g of salt, and 1 beaten egg to the mixture and continue to stir until a thick batter is obtained;
- Place the mixture in a container greased with oil and refrigerate it for about an hour to rest;
- Prepare balls of about 70 g in weight, cover them with cling film and let them rise for about 4 hours;
- In the meantime, prepare the ricotta cream:
- Put 500 g of ricotta in a large, tight-meshed sieve and let it drain for a few hours in the refrigerator, then pass it through a sieve a couple of times;
- Mix the ricotta with a whisk together with 180 g of sugar;
- Add 50 g of chocolate chips and place the mixture in a pastry bag in the refrigerator for at least an hour;
- Once they have risen, flatten the balls with your fingers and roll them on themselves by stretching them, trying to obtain loaves of about 30 cm /12" in length;
- Roll up the strips of dough obtained on the aluminum cylinders for cannoli, trying to fit the ends under the dough and let it rise for another hour;
- Put plenty of peanut oil in a pan of 20 cm /8" in diameter and heat it up to 170°C / 340°F then dip the packets in it two at a time and fry them until golden brown (always keep under control the temperature of the oil that must remain on the 170°C / 340°F);
- Leave them for a few seconds on absorbent kitchen paper so that they lose excess oil, then remove the cylinder and roll each packet (still hot) in the granulated sugar, then set them aside to cool;
- Fill the packets with plenty of ricotta cream just before serving.

If you prefer, you can bake your parcels in the oven: 15-20 minutes at 180°C / 355°F in a preheated static oven. In this case, the granulated sugar would not stick, so sprinkle them once lukewarm with powdered sugar.

10.5 – Filled fragrant fried pastry

Ingredients

- 120 g of mother yeast
- 400 g of very strong (strong bread) flour
- 80 g of plain (all purpose) flour
- 80 g of caster sugar
- 80 g of butter at room temperature
- 100 ml of milk
- 2 eggs
- 1 pinch of salt
- Peanut oil for frying
- Classic or chocolate custard (find the recipe in chapter 3)

Directions

- Put 120 g of mother yeast in 100 ml of warm milk with 80 g of sugar in the bowl of the mixer and start mixing;
- Once the yeast is dissolved, add 2 eggs one at a time, 1 pinch of salt and continue kneading;
- Add 80 g of plain flour and 400 g of very strong flour a little at a time and continue to knead so as to incorporate it all;
- Once the dough comes off the sides of the bowl, add 80 g of soft butter cut into small pieces a little at a time, checking that the previous ones have been well absorbed before inserting

the next, and knead until you get a soft and elastic dough and not sticky;

- Form a ball and let it rise in the heat for 4-5 hours until doubled;
- In the meantime, prepare the classic or chocolate custard following the recipe you find in chapter 3, it will be a fabulous filling! (You can also use jam to taste or Nutella, if you prefer);
- Once the dough has risen, divide it into 4 or more loaves, so that subsequent processing is easier;
- Roll out a portion of the dough with a rolling pin or better still with the homemade pasta machine, obtaining a thin but not transparent sheet;
- Place it on a lightly floured work surface, and with a teaspoon place piles of custard equally spaced;
- Apply another sheet of the same size on the first one and cut with a wheel making sure that the filling remains in the center of them (the shape is not important, you can indulge yourself with shapes and sizes, it is important that it always has the same thickness);
- Repeat this operation until all the ingredients are used up;
- In a saucepan with high sides, heat the peanut oil over medium-high heat and when it is hot enough (about 180°C / 355°F) dip the stuffed pastries a few at a time and turn them until golden on both sides;
- Once cooked, drain on absorbent paper, place them on a serving dish and sprinkle with powdered sugar

10.6 – Fried pastry dough

Ingredients

- 150 g of mother yeast
- 160 g of mixed grain flour
- 240 g of very strong (strong bread) flour
- 40 g of butter at room temperature
- 2 eggs
- 1 egg yolk
- 55 g of caster sugar
- 20 ml dry marsala (liqueur)
- 1 vanilla bean
- 1 vial of lemon or orange flavoring (or essential oil)
- 1 pinch of salt

Directions

- Put 150 g of mother yeast together with 55 g of sugar, 2 eggs, 1 egg yolk in the bowl of the mixer and start mixing;
- Once the yeast is dissolved, add the vanilla, 1 pinch of salt, 1 vial of lemon or orange flavoring, 160 g of mixed grain flour and continue kneading;
- Add 20 ml of dry marsala, 240 g of flour a little at a time and continue to knead in order to incorporate it and obtain a homogeneous mixture;

- Once the dough comes off the sides of the bowl, add 40 g of soft butter cut into small pieces a little at a time, checking that the previous one has been well absorbed before inserting the next. Knead until a soft and elastic dough is obtained, not sticky;
- Form a ball, let it rest for 1 hour and then place it in an airtight container in the fridge for 24 hours;
- At this point, divide the dough into 2 or more loaves so that processing is easier;
- Roll out a portion of the dough with a rolling pin or better still with the homemade pasta machine, obtaining a thin but not transparent sheet;
- Cut into strips or shapes of dough as desired using a knurled wheel, and place them on a lightly floured work surface and cover with a cloth;
- Let them rest for about 15 minutes, in the meantime heat an abundant amount of peanut oil in a saucepan;
- Once it reaches a temperature of about 170 ° C / 340 ° F, immerse the dough, turning them on both sides to cook evenly;
- Once golden, put them to dry on absorbent paper. Place them on a serving dish and sprinkle them with powdered sugar.

Chapter 11

(Almost) Large leavened products

11.1 – Easy mini "panettone"

Ingredients

- 60 g of mother yeast
- 140 g of very strong (strong bread) flour
- 45 g of caster sugar
- 70 g of water
- 2 egg yolks
- 45 g of softened butter
- 18 g of acacia honey
- 70 g of sultanas
- 50 g of candied orange
- The zest of 1/2 lemon
- The zest of 1/2 orange
- 1 vanilla bean
- Cupcake molds

Direction

- Put 60 g of mother yeast with 70 ml of water in the bowl of the mixer, and start kneading;
- Add 140 g of flour, 18 g of acacia honey, vanilla and stir until the mixture is combined;

- Now add 45 g of sugar a little at a time, so as to incorporate it slowly (during the whole mixing phase check that the dough temperature never exceeds 26°C / 79°F; in this case, put the dough in the fridge to cool before proceeding);
- When it is absorbed, add 25 g of butter and then 20 g more to incorporate it slowly;
- Continue adding to the dough 2 egg yolks, one at a time, and knead until they are absorbed;
- At this point, turn on the planetary mixer for about 5 minutes until the dough is smooth, homogeneous and strung;
- Add 70 g of sultanas, 50 g of candied orange, the zest of 1/2 lemon, the zest of 1/2 orange and stir for a few seconds so that they are distributed well in the dough;
- Turn the mass over on the work surface and let it rest for 1 hour covered with a cloth;
- Divide it into portions of about 60 g (it depends on the size of your cupcake mold). Reinforce them by giving them a spherical shape and let them rest again for another 30 minutes;
- Place them into the paper cup inside the cupcake mold and cover them with cling film;
- Put them to rise in a warm place (about 25°C / 77°F, inside the oven with the light on, if necessary) for 8-10 hours until doubled in volume;
- Once they have risen, uncover them delicately, make a cross incision on the surface, and place a very small knob of butter on it;
- Bake the mini panettone in a preheated oven at 180°C / 355°F for 30 minutes or until they reach a core temperature of 94°C / 201°F.

11.2 – Easy chocolate panettone cake

Ingredients

- 80 g of mother yeast
- 250 g of very strong (strong bread) flour
- 70 ml of water
- 40 g of caster sugar
- 30 g of honey
- 2 eggs
- 100 g of melted butter
- 1 pinch of salt
- 1 vanilla bean
- 50 g of sultanas
- 70 g of dark chocolate

Ingredients for a 500 g mold

Directions

- Mix 80 g of mother yeast with 70 ml of water, 40 g of sugar and 30 g of honey until the wild yeast is dissolved;
- Add 250 g of flour, 1 pinch of salt, vanilla and stir until all the ingredients are homogeneous;
- Add 100 g of melted butter (at room temperature) divided in two, in order to incorporate it slowly;

- Continue adding 2 eggs, one at a time, and knead until they are absorbed;
- At this point, turn on the planetary mixer for about 5 minutes until the dough is smooth, homogeneous and strung (the dough will be very soft but don't worry);
- Finally add 50 g of sultanas, 70 g of chopped dark chocolate and stir for a few seconds so that they are distributed in the dough;
- Leave to rise for about 6 hours, or until doubled in volume, in a warm place and covered with clingfilm;
- Now turn the dough upside down on a board and start making reinforcing folds, folding it on itself a couple of times in different directions (slowly the dough will string);
- At this point, place the dough in an airtight container in the fridge overnight (about 8 hours);
- Resume kneading the dough by making reinforcing folds to obtain a strung dough, smooth and without lumps (check by testing the veil);
- Give it a round shape, put it in a 500 g mold and cover it with plastic wrap;
- Leave the panettone to rise in the heat for about 8 hours until it reaches 2 cm / 0.8" from the edge of the mold;
- Bake in a hot oven for 3-4 minutes at approximately 220°C / 340°F, then lower the oven to 160°C / 320°F and bake for another 40 minutes. (This way, the oven should remain hot without the resistances turning on. If you see the top of panettone cooking too quickly, cover it with aluminum foil).
- The panettone will be completely cooked when the heart reaches a temperature of 94°C / 201°F, then take it out of the oven and let it cool well on a grill, or even better, upside down stuck with the special pins;
- When it is completely cold, close it in a plastic food bag for at least 24 hours (if you can resist, consume the panettone a few days later, it will be even tastier).

11.3 – Easy laminated pandoro cake

Ingredients

First dough:
- 100 g of mother yeast
- 75 g of very strong (or bread strong) flour
- 2 eggs
- 45 g of caster sugar
- 10 g of honey
- 30 g of high-quality butter at room temperature

Second dough:
- First dough
- 190 + 75 g of very strong (or bread strong) flour
- 1 egg
- 4 egg yolks
- 65 g of caster sugar
- 1 vanilla bean
- 10 g of salt

Lamination:
- 30 g of high-quality butter

Ingredients for a 750 g pandoro cake mold

Directions

For the preparation of the first dough, I recommend starting at 4 pm.

- Put 100 g of mother yeast and 75 g of flour in the bowl of the mixer and start mixing;
- Add 2 eggs, one at a time, continuing to knead until they are absorbed, then add 45 g of sugar a little at a time and 10 g of honey;
- When you have obtained a homogeneous mixture, add 30 g of melted and cooled butter a little at a time;
- Continue to knead at medium speed until the dough is strung;
- Leave it to rise in an airtight container in the oven that is turned off with the light on for one night (10 hours);
- The following day it should be more than doubled but if it isn't, wait until it is, then start making the second dough:
- In the bowl of the planetary mixer, add 190 g of flour to the main dough and start kneading;
- Then insert 1 egg and 3 yolks one at a time, alternating them with 65 g of sugar;
- When the mixture is smooth and homogeneous, add the vanilla, 10 g of salt, and 75 g of remaining flour a little at a time;
- Continue to spin the hook at medium speed for a few minutes until the dough is nice and smooth and strung (do the veil test);
- Place the dough in an airtight container and let it rise in the oven with the light on for 7-8 hours until it has tripled;
- Then, place the dough on a floured surface, do reinforcing folds, and repeat the operation twice, one every 20 minutes, until the dough is strung again (you need to obtain a strung dough, smooth and without lumps - check by testing the veil);
- Let the dough rest for at least 1 hour at room temperature;
- Begin the lamination process. If you have any doubts about how to perform a good lamination, consult chapter 4 dedicated to lamination baked products, where I explain all the steps. In this case, however, the intent is not to obtain a flaky product, but that of distributing a large amount of butter evenly, without having to add it during the kneading phase as it makes the leavening phase slower;

- Work the dough to obtain a square of about 15 x 15 cm / 6x6", then press with a rolling pin in the center of it, making a cross perpendicular to the sides;
- Now roll out the four portions of dough obtained individually in order to obtain 4 tongues of dough, but leaving the central part thicker;
- Place 200 g of cold butter in thin slices on the thickest central part and fold the tongues previously spread over it, in order to trap it;
- Leave the mass to rest for at least half an hour in the fridge, then give two rounds of dough with three folds, putting the dough in the fridge between one fold and the other, making the next round only when the butter is hardened again;
- Perform the last sheeting with a "4 fold" (again, check chapter 4), then form a ball and place it in the 750 g pandoro mold previously greased and floured;
- Cover it and let it rise in the oven with the light on for about 4 hours until it has almost reached the edge of the mold;
- Bake in the lower part of the oven in static mode, preheated to 170°C / 340°F for the first 10 minutes, then lower the temperature to 160°C / 320°F and let it bake for another 30 minutes until it reaches a temperature of 94°C / 200°F in the pandoro core (if the surface tends to darken too much, cover it with aluminium foil);
- Once cooked, let it cool for at least 1 hour. At this point, turn the pandoro over on a grid, removing the mold and letting it cool for at least another 10 hours covered with a clean cloth.

It can be stored in a cellophane bag for up to 15 days

11.4 – The genoese "pandolce"

Ingredients
First dough:
- 120 g of mother yeast
- 240 g of very strong (strong bread) flour
- 40 ml of water
- 1 vial of orange flavoring
- 1 egg yolk
- 55 g of cold melted butter
- 55 g of caster sugar

Second dough:
- First dough
- 40 g of very strong (strong bread) flour
- 15 g of caster sugar
- 15 ml of limoncino
- 1 pinch of salt
- 20 g of butter

Filling
- 240 g of sultanas
- 1 tablespoon of pine nuts
- 65 g of candied fruit (cedar, diced orange)
- Fennel seeds (optional)

- Marsala or limoncino to soak the raisins

Ingredients for a 850 g panettone cake mold

Directions

First dough:

- Mix 120 g of mother yeast with 40 ml of water and 55 g of sugar until the yeast is dissolved;
- Combine 240 g of flour, 1 egg yolk, 1 vial of orange flavoring and continue kneading;
- Now add 55 g of cold melted butter a little at a time until it is completely incorporated;
- Let it run for several minutes until the mixture is smooth, homogeneous and strung;
- Place it in a large bowl, cover it with cling film and let it rise for about 8 hours until the dough has tripled its volume (one night).

The day after, start making the second dough:

- Put the dough back into the bowl of the mixer and add 40 g of flour, 15 g of sugar, 15 ml of marsala (or limoncino) and operate the hook;
- Turn it for a few minutes, adding the softened butter, cut into small pieces, a little at a time (you need to obtain a strung, smooth and lump-free dough - check it by testing the veil);
- In the meantime, soak 240 g of sultanas in Marsala (or water, if you wish) for half an hour, then squeeze it well and add it to the dough;
- Also add 1 tablespoon of pine nuts, 65 g of candied fruit (cedar, diced orange), fennel seeds (optional) and mix everything (I prefer to do it by hand out of the mixer on a lightly floured surface);
- Proceed with the so-called "pirlatura" which consists in turning the dough in your hands to give the classic round shape to the "pandolce";

- With a knife, make a cut in the shape of a triangle deep enough on the surface of the "pandolce", as tradition dictates;
- Place it on a baking sheet lined with baking paper and let it rise for another 4-5 hours covered with cling film; (To prevent the "pandolce" from flattening too much, I recommend that you close it inside a circle of parchment paper of about 19 cm /7" in diameter, which you will remove once it is baked)
- Once doubled, bake the "pandolce" at 180°C / 355°F for 40-45 minutes until golden brown. Check the cooking and if it gets too dark on the surface cover it with an aluminium foil and lower the temperature;
- Once cooked, let it cool for at least 1 hour, then leave it for at least another 8 hours covered with a clean cloth.

It can be stored in a cellophane bag for up to 15 days.

Made in the USA
Monee, IL
21 December 2023

50151872R00109